Television, sex roles and children

Television, sex roles and children:
A developmental social psychological account

Kevin Durkin

OPEN UNIVERSITY PRESS

Milton Keynes · Philadelphia

Open University Press
Open University Educational Enterprises Limited
12 Cofferidge Close
Stony Stratford
Milton Keynes MK11 1BY, England
and
242 Cherry Street
Philadelphia, PA 19106, USA

First Published 1985

British Library Cataloguing in Publication Data
Durkin, Kevin
    Television, sex roles and children: a developmental social
    psychological account.
    1. Sex role in children   2. Television and children
    I. Title
    305.2'3   BF723.S42

    ISBN 0-335-15069-1
    ISBN 0-335-15068-3 Pbk

Library of Congress Cataloging in Publication Data
Durkin, Kevin
    Television, sex roles, and children.
    Bibliography: p.
    Includes indexes.
    1. Television and children. 2. Sex role in television
3. Stereotype (Psychology) I. Title.
HQ784.T4D88 1985   305.2'3   85-13629

ISBN 0-335-15069-1
ISBN 0-335-15068-3 (pbk.)

Text design by Nicola Sheldon
Photoset by Rowland Phototypesetting Limited
Bury St Edmunds, Suffolk
Printed in Great Britain by
J. W. Arrowsmith Limited, Bristol

To my mother, Alice Durkin,
and to the memory of my father,
Tom Durkin

Contents

Acknowledgments

My own research into television and sex role acquisition, some of which is summarized here, was supported by a grant from the Independent Broadcasting Authority, London. Although I bear responsibility for any views or opinions I express relating to that work, and no endorsement by the funding agency should be inferred, it would not have been possible without the generous support that the I.B.A. provided. I am grateful to the I.B.A. Research Department, in particular, to Dr Mallory Wober who acted as official contact during the project and provided invaluable encouragement, information and professional contacts throughout the work, and to Dr Barrie Gunter, for informal and informed advice at several points.

More generally, my work and my thinking about the media and sex roles have been developed as a member of the Social Psychology Research Unit, University of Kent. I am grateful to many friends and colleagues in the Unit for direct and indirect support, but particularly to Geoffrey Stephenson for encouraging my research in communications and media, to Derek Rutter for general support, to Beatrice Shire for being Canterbury's Pied Piper on wheels, to Rupert Brown for raising typically awkward questions that made me think more carefully about some of the arguments presented here in Chapter 6, to Maryon Tysoe, for making some of this work a 'finding', and to John Caputo, for providing the view from Euphoric State.

Some of the ideas presented in this book are developed and revised from papers I have published in the *British Journal of Social Psychology*, *Communication Research* and the *Journal of Educational Television*, and I am very grateful to the Editors and reviewers of these periodicals for the feedback and advice I received from them. I am also indebted to Tony Manstead, University of Manchester, for encouragement and advice he gave selflessly at an early stage of my interest in television and sex roles.

Sheila Sullivan and Debbie Winters typed successive drafts of the manuscript with their customary skills, speed and resilience in the face of my handwriting.

I am very grateful to John Skelton and Pat Lee at Open University Press for the friendly and supportive climate they foster for their authors. I am indebted, too, to the three anonymous reviewers for Open University Press, whose constructive comments helped fashion the final version.

Finally, I am grateful to Parvin Akhtar-Durkin, for inordinate help at just about every stage of this work. I cannot list everything she has contributed and cannot summarize everything I owe to her. Suffice it to say that she will always preserve me from the down side of gender aschematism.

Kevin Durkin
February 1985
Canterbury

Introduction

Television is now established as the foremost leisure activity of a large proportion of the world's population. In the more affluent countries, almost every home possesses at least one set, and it is viewed regularly by virtually all members of the family, often for several hours per day. Children are particularly devoted to the medium, in many cases passing proportionately greater amounts of their waking hours in front of the TV than do adults, and spending more time with the TV than in the classroom.

Not surprisingly, parents, politicians and social scientists alike have frequently asked what might be the effects on the young of growing up in a television culture, where one mass medium has the unprecedented power to reach simultaneously into the living rooms of every household and to present so vividly selected images of events and lifestyles that are often depicted for their entertainment value rather than their social desirability. In so far as considerations of social desirability impinge upon the work of broadcasters, much of the focus to date has been on the issue of television violence. The consequences to children of viewing violence has been the subject of countless research studies and still greater amounts of speculation during the last three decades.

But it has also been recognized since the earliest research studies in this field that the scope of TV content is so broad as to touch on most aspects of human lives (cf. Himmelweit *et al.* 1958; Schramm *et al.* 1961), and in recent years interest has increased in the possible involvement of TV in several areas of child development. In the

1970s, greater interest was being shown in the possible *pro*social capacities of TV, teaching the values of cooperation, sharing and altruism (Huston-Stein and Friedrich 1975) and in the educational potential of TV, as a medium equipped to hold the attention of youngsters with its unique presentational techniques so that learning can be readily enjoyable (see Greenfield 1984). Considerable creative and research energy has been devoted to the production and testing of television materials for children aimed at more constructive ends than the dubious delights of watching *Popeye* beat *Bluto* to pulp.

The interests of mass media professionals and of research workers reflect in part the developments in the societies around them, and one major development in Western societies over the last 15 years or so has been the widespread reconsideration of the constraints upon human behaviour and opportunities due to the maintenance of traditional sex roles. Changes in the employment structures of Western economies, political lobbying towards equal rights for women, the growth of feminism, and increasing deferment of marriage among younger generations have all contributed towards an uneasy and incomplete transition in contemporary thinking about male and female roles.

These developments have had consequences within the mass media, where pressure groups and individuals have fought for greater representation of women in the senior levels of the organizations, and where some writers have included non-traditional themes and arguments in their productions. Needless to say, the changes cannot be claimed to be sweeping and they have neither reached all levels of media output nor been couched in a climate wholly conducive to egalitarianism. The media's interests in sex generally revolve more around sensuality and sensationalism than matters of human rights, and it is not difficult to find instances of trivialization and distortion in the discussion and reportage of sex role issues in most of the mass media.

Critics of the media frequently complain of the perpetuation of sex role stereotypes therein, and it is this topic in particular which has engaged the greatest amount of relevant research interest in recent years. Numerous studies of content have confirmed what critical viewers have long suspected, that the media in general are quite biased in the ways they present males and females. Understandably, this awareness has fuelled concern about the impact of what many see as rampant sexism in the media upon those still learning about their own roles and potentialities – the young. Correspondingly, those concerned with the prospects for change have asked what consequences there may be upon the introduction of television images which are not sex typed and which defy or reverse traditional roles.

As a result, a new wave of research activity is currently under way, and investigators are now examining the content of sex role images in the mass media and the ways in which they affect viewers, especially, but not exclusively, children. The effects of changes are being tested as well. This research is still very much in its early stages in comparison with work on media violence, and the findings are by no means as extensive, but it is growing and it addresses topics of such far-reaching importance to the study of human society that it is likely to continue to grow. Not all human beings engage in the pursuit of violence, but all are assigned membership of a gender category, and in most cases this membership has fundamental implications for the individual's life. The possible relationships between sex role development and the content of the primary mass medium, television, alongside which most children spend tens of thousands of their formative hours, are self-evidently deserving of careful scrutiny.

The goals of this book are to assemble and to evaluate the main findings of recent work on television and sex role acquisition, to point to gaps and limitations in present enquiry, and to sketch a framework around which future research might usefully address some of the remaining questions. The book is aimed at students in the social sciences and mass communications, and the author's perspective is that of a developmental social psychologist. Thus, a main focus of the book will be on the ways in which developing social beings take account of information and social influences in the world around them, and an overriding theme will be that rather than *assume* TV has or does not have a particular effect upon children, we need to *investigate* the matter. As I hope to make clear, the investigation to date, and the complexities of the viewer – medium relationship at stake, are such that assumptions of simple effects do not carry us very far. For this reason, declaring that the book is addressed to students is not a euphemism for a promise to avoid difficult issues.

Consequently, I ought to forewarn the reader that the argument that TV is sex stereotyped and therefore its effects are to induce or 'condition' sex stereotyping in the young is *not* what lies in store in the following pages. We will be examining this hypothesis and its variants, but it will be argued that it is theoretically deficient and empirically unsupported. My theme will be that television may be implicated in the sex role development of children in different ways at different points in the lifespan, that as much depends upon what the child brings to TV viewing as upon what it extracts, and that to understand any of these processes calls for sophisticated theory and research – much of which has still to be formulated. Hence, I hope that some of the students who read this text will find within it questions to pursue rather than confirmation of a naive hypothesis that has current popularity but little explanatory power. Apart from correspondence here and there with the known complexity of child development, my excuse for this pedantry is that I believe that for both theoretical and practical reasons sex role acquisition is a very important aspect of people's lives, and that to make casual assumptions about how it proceeds without venturing to test them is a poor basis for understanding and for change.

Some notice of the book's limitations ought to be given here. Although as I have indicated, sex stereotyping is not confined to television, and although we cannot suppose sex roles to be irrelevant to the lives of people beyond childhood, the book will be concerned primarily with the one medium and with child viewers only. The first restriction is partly because the ubiquity and accessibility of TV make it the most widely consumed mass medium and, therefore, attention worthy in its own right. It is also partly because there are good reasons for supposing that different media involve different processing capacities in the viewer (Salomon 1979; Greenfield 1984). Thus, while many of the issues to be discussed here do overlap with the study of other media, attention will be restricted to television partly because of its pre-eminence among its neighbours, partly for the sake of organizational convenience, and partly because of the limited availability of work comparing the effects of exposure to sex stereotyping in different forms of media. Even so, it will be obvious to any media user that materials from one may appear in another: in the words of Kington (1983:67), the cinema has become 'a place where you can get a preview of a television film', and of course many personalities (such as musicians) can be encountered in various media. 'Television' will therefore be treated here as a fuzzy category to allow for its interrelationship with other forms of entertainment, but it should be stressed that each medium has its own way of conveying ideas and images and the consumer's response may vary correspondingly.

While the impact of media stereotypes on adults is of course an important topic and ultimately inseparable from a fully developmental account, only a very few relevant studies are presently available using adult viewers and there is not enough evidence yet to attempt a (much-needed) lifespan account. (The reader interested in pursuing this independently is referred to Butler and Paisley (1980), Ross *et al.* (1982), Gunter and Wober (1982), Geis *et al.* (1984), and Durkin (in press) for some relevant material and further references.)

It should also be emphasized that this book is concerned with aspects of the medium–viewer relationship rather than with how the medium comes to adopt the characteristics (specifically, the sexist bias) that it has. The mass media in general tend to be male-dominated enterprises (Eddings 1980; Butler and Paisley 1980) and in this respect seem to bear more than a coincidental relationship to the nature of the surrounding society. As Dorr Leifer *et al.* (1974:227–8) point out, television producers are as likely as many other members of the community to have sex stereotyped views about the kind of programme content that the public in general, and children in particular, will wish to see, and middle class male writers are likely to find it easier to compose material about people like themselves. Clearly, the medium as an industry reflects aspects of the culture that supports it, but it is not the purpose of this book to reiterate points that have already been well made on this relationship by others (see, e.g. Eddings (1980) and Butler and Paisley (1980) on institutional sexism in the media).

Finally, reference to the broader society reminds us that television is scarcely alone in whatever contribution it makes to the perpetuation of sex role stereotypes. Virtually every other mass medium exhibits traditional stereotypes, and virtually every social institution, from the family and the peer group to the school and the occupational world, offers different opportunities and expectations to people according to their gender. Societies managed to uphold traditional sex role divisions before the arrival of television and many continue to do so in its absence. No social scientist would attribute responsibility for sex role stratification uniquely to television. Nevertheless, this medium has occasioned such a far-reaching transformation of the communication systems of modern societies and now holds such a prominent position in the daily lives of so many people, that the social worlds into which contemporary children are arriving are qualitatively distinguished by its presence. It is valid to ask what place it has in the ways these generations gather their social knowledge, and it would be patently absurd not to study television on the grounds that some people do not have one.

There are pitfalls in trying to examine one variable at a time when analysing multi-determined phenomena such as sex roles, and we will see throughout the text that there are good reasons to attend to other factors, but before we explain the universe we need carefully to assess its parts. The study of television and sex role acquisition is a small, but interesting, contribution to a larger endeavour.

In Chapter 1, some key terms will be defined and some influential theoretical perspectives on how the mass media relate to society will be discussed. Chapter 2 describes the sex role content of television, based on a review of a large number of recent analyses of this aspect of the medium. Before examining the evidence on how children react to this content, the main theories of sex role acquisition will be considered in Chapter 3, in order to provide an overview of the breadth of the developmental issues at stake. In Chapter 4, the evidence pertaining to one particular hypothesis, specifically that the more TV children watch, the more sex stereotyped their own beliefs become, will be reviewed – and found lacking. Chapter 5 argues that a more productive way of examining the relationship between children and

TV sex role images is to look at how children set about interpreting what they watch. Evidence that children's existing abilities and beliefs predetermine many of the effects of television will be discussed in Chapter 5, and also in Chapter 6, when we turn to young people's reactions to non-traditional, or counterstereotyped, programmes. Finally, in Chapter 7, some of the (many) remaining questions for future research will be summarized, and I will attempt to indicate why the most promising framework within which to pursue such work is that of a developmental social psychology.

ONE

Sex roles and television: concepts and theories

Every man knows the feelings of that tense approach to the shabby exterior of some rented room in a Lower East Side apartment building, gingerly setting his gun, crashing through the door, slamming hard against the inside wall with the weapon fixed on the first thing that moves. Only to find that the moving object bears a striking resemblance to Marilyn Monroe, doesn't appear to own a complete set of pyjamas, and clearly feels that this is the right moment in her life to abandon a long-term policy of coolness towards male strangers.

Every woman regularly faces comparable social demands. If Mr Right is not leaping into her bedroom as a side-stop on the route to bullet-spewing glory, he will pop up, dripping with the accoutrements of mega-wealth, in restaurants, tennis clubs, or backstage as she leaves the chorus line, and fight for her hand (or other parts, depending upon the lateness of the broadcast) in the face of all obstacles and rivals.

It is easy to scoff at these familiar television fantasies, and it is easy to recall other well-worn scenarios: the family in perpetual Christmas with Dad lavishing football kits on the boys and trinkets on his little girl, while Mum merrily knocks up another round of cocoa in the kitchen, or those relentless heroes still battling away in World War II, leaving tearful females in their wake as they climb the skies for a spot of single-handed dispersement of the enemy air force. It would take quite a lot of channel-hopping to spend an evening with the TV without being stuck into the antics of assertive men and decorative women cast in something like these moulds.

Anybody with a television set recognizes these recurring themes and images. We know as viewers that much of what we watch will include some instance or variation upon them. Any person who is television literate can predict the broad route a programme will follow once he or she has seen the main characters and grasped the basics of the plot or story. Have you ever watched a film in which a man meets a woman, they fall in love, suffer some misunderstanding or transient threat to the relationship, recover and are last seen planning a marriage and showing every prospect of living happily ever after? It is probably more difficult to recall a film in which this *does not* happen, if not as the central theme, then at least as a subsidiary line.

Of course, there have always been exceptions to the routine on television. Certainly, the contemporary viewer has a slightly greater chance than she or he would have had ten years ago of switching on and finding that it is someone like Mary Beth Cagney hunting criminals in the seamier districts of New York City, or of discovering *Mr* Kramer fighting to keep his kid, or of seeing a soap opera husband affronted that his wife has decided to take up a career of her own. But these departures from tradition are noteworthy because of their still relatively unusual status, and much of the TV diet remains along the lines sketched above: a regular and generous display of traditional sex-role stereotypes.

This book is about the reactions of children to these stereotyped themes and images, and about the possible consequences of changing TV content. In subsequent chapters, I will review the research evidence on the sex role *content* of TV and go on to explore its possible effects upon young viewers. Later, I will examine research concerned with the results of showing children counterstereotyped television material. It will be useful first to consider what is meant by some of the key terms used throughout the book, beginning with the terms *sex role*, *sex role stereotype* and *sexism*. I will then consider in broad outline some of the ways in which psychologists and communications researchers have set about studying the relationship between mass media and society.

One preliminary point is that I will use the words *sex* and *gender* interchangeably in this book. Some researchers argue persuasively for a distinction between these, taking one to refer to biological category and the other to refer to a sociocultural construction. While there are important conceptual issues at stake here (see Archer and Lloyd (1982) for a relevant discussion), even researchers agreed on the theoretical point sometimes differ on the terminological one: some investigators use the term 'gender' to refer to biological sex, and reserve the term 'sex roles' for the sociocultural sense (e.g. Spence and Helmreich 1978), while others use the terms in the opposite way, so that 'gender' refers to the social construct and 'sex' to the biological fact (e.g. Archer and Lloyd 1982). By using the words interchangeably, I do not intend to imply disregard for the conceptual distinction but simply to accept that the distinction between labels is not established in our dictionaries, nor settled yet in scientific terminology.

Sex role

The term sex role refers to the collection of behaviours or activities that a given society deems more appropriate to members of one sex than to members of the other sex. In some societies, sex roles are quite rigidly prescribed with a dichotomy strictly maintained between, say, a male role of head of family and breadwinner, and a female role of wife and mother. Most societies have traditionally organized sex roles around duties such as these, according greater economic autonomy and responsibilities to the male, and greater domestic obligations to the female, though these tend to be probabilistic rather than absolute divisions in contemporary Western societies. In the latter there are many overlaps in roles between the sexes, but sex nevertheless is associated with powerful public expectations and endorsement of particular patterns of behaviour. For example, authoritative and constructive activities, such as running an organization or repairing machinery, are predominantly (but not exclusively) undertaken by men, while nurturing and domestic activities, such as looking after small children or doing routine home cooking, are predominantly (but not exclusively) undertaken by women. Strictly speaking, we are referring here to age – sex roles; not all sex-related expectations are constant through childhood to old age (for example, we would not expect a 5-year-old boy to take masterful charge of his mother, an elderly grandfather to be as tough and assertive as a 24-year-old man beginning his family responsibilities, etc.) but, age for age, there are usually detectable differences in what is deemed appropriate for a male versus a female. In short, in areas of work, leisure and interpersonal relationships, specific ways of behaving are more likely to be adopted by and expected of members of a specific sex. To the extent that this happens in a given society, it is a manifestation of the allocation of sex roles in that society.

It should be stressed that sex roles are 'public', in the sense that they are observable patterns of behaviour, manifest in various ways in actions, relationships, style of appearance, overt personal goals, and so on. The sexes can be distinguished around these criteria in most societies (though, as already suggested, some communities are more rigid than others). The relationship between these relatively external characteristics and the relatively internal ones, such as intellect and personality attributes, however, is not as straightforward as may first appear to be the case, and as traditional beliefs might lead one to suppose. There is little evidence of systematic or substantial differences in intellectual capacities between the sexes (e.g. Fairweather 1976; Archer and Lloyd 1982; Nicholson 1984). Similarly, when personality psychologists look carefully at the extent to which individual males and females possess characteristics traditionally thought of as 'masculine' or 'feminine', they find that people do not fall into dichotomies whereby all men are 'leaderlike', 'aggressive', 'willing to take risks', *etc.*, and all females are 'affectionate', 'gentle', 'sympathetic', *etc.* Clearly, individuals of *either* sex may possess some or all of these (and other supposedly masculine or feminine) characteristics. Work on these aspects of personality have led many researchers (e.g. Constantinople 1973; Bem 1974; Spence and Helmreich 1978) to abandon the traditional view that masculinity and femininity are bipolar opposites, and to see these as labels for qualities which can be found to varying degrees in most individuals.

Measures such as the Bem Sex Role Inventory (BSRI) are now widely used by psychologists to gauge the extent to which a person reports her or himself as possessing masculine or feminine characteristics, and of course different individuals show different distributions of these properties.

Conceivably, individuals of either sex may in some situations choose to inhibit certain personal features: a woman may have the capacity to be leaderlike but may find negative reactions from others sufficiently uncomfortable to make her repress this potential; a man may experience emotional distress but be loath to display it. This suspected discrepancy between underlying personal characteristics and social constraints, i.e. between the broad complexity of any individual's personality and the sex role which is particularly expected of her or him, leads to the conjecture that for many people aspects of their sex role may be incompatible with their full personal development. Correspondingly, some individuals may lack some of the traits associated with the role for their sex (for example, some males may not feel competitive, and some females may not feel nurturant towards children), yet feel obliged to present signs of these in certain contexts as they 'act out' their allotted parts. Sex roles, then, are what are *expected* of us, and their relationship to what we *are*, or might wish to be, is not always straightforward.

Sex role stereotypes

While sex role differences occur and are very important aspects of the way our societies are organized, the stress on the probabilistic dimension above reflects the fact that in actuality there is considerable overlap of personal roles, and many cases exist of individuals engaging in behaviours that are more often undertaken by the opposite sex. For example, it is not impossible to find some powerful female political figures, or some men whose occupations are in the caring professions, or some girls who enjoy rough and tumble games more than their brothers, and so on. What *is* more rigid, however, is the constellation of beliefs and expectations held by members of a society about the capacities and preferences of the sexes. These generalized beliefs about what is appropriate to and typical of a particular sex constitute *sex role stereotypes*.

A useful definition of sex role stereotypes is that of Ashmore and Del Boca (1979:222), who describe them as the structured sets of beliefs about the personal attributes of women and men. This definition captures the general agreement of social psychologists interested in the study of stereotypes that they are organized cognitive structures that facilitate the categorization and simplification of the social environment. It should be stressed that at this level stereotyping is no more or less than a neutral cognitive mechanism which we all exploit in attempting to discern consistency in a complex world. Just as we organize our beliefs about what the weather will be like in January, so we organize our beliefs about what members of a given social category will be like. It would be very difficult to interact in a large society if we were unable to make use of these cognitive guidelines in anticipating and predicting the properties of other people.

The second emphasis of Ashmore and Del Boca's definition, 'personal attributes', is intended to take account of the fact that our structured sets of beliefs about people cover physical properties, personality characteristics and behavioural patterns. That is, once we have a stereotype for a particular group we have expectations not only of what its members will look like, but also of their 'underlying' traits and of the ways in which they are likely to behave in certain situations. Williams and Best (1982:16) draw a further distinction in this respect between sex *role* stereotypes, which they see as being concerned with activities, and sex *trait* stereotypes, which 'consist of those psychological characteristics or behavioural traits that are believed to characterize men with much greater (or lesser) frequency than they characterize women'. For present purposes, it will be taken that trait stereotypes can be subsumed within role stereotypes, as defined by

Ashmore and Del Boca, but the distinction is worth recording because it will be seen later in the book to be relevant to the ways in which researchers have analysed sex role content in television.

I will not attempt here to review the field of research concerned with uncovering the details of contemporary sex role stereotypes. For convenience, I will assume, like others (e.g. Deaux 1976:13f.), that they include the ascription to men of traits such as independence, objectivity, competitiveness, assertiveness and ambition, and to women of traits such as dependence, emotionality, nurturance and preoccupation with physical appearance. They include the expectation that men will strive for dominance and achievement, and that women will opt for compliance and support. We could debate and dissect these, and it is worth pointing out that the existing tests of stereotypes are not entirely satisfactory (see Sayers (1979) for further discussion). It is also the case that we have more than one stereotype per sex (viz. the housewife, the career woman, the feminist, the dumb blonde, the businessman, the stud, the breadwinner, the strong silent type, and so on), but the core stereotypes serve our present purposes by summarizing recognizable sets of traditional beliefs about the sexes. In Chapter 2, we will look in more detail at the sex role stereotypes presented in contemporary television. Notice for the moment that the elements of sex role stereotypes indicated here inevitably emphasize differences rather than similarities between the sexes, and they tend to be focused upon relatively *extreme* features (see McArthur (1982) for a more general discussion of this aspect of stereotypes).

One other essential point about stereotypes is developed by the social psychologist Tajfel (1981), who stresses that important questions are missed if we confine analysis to the cognitive components of these belief structures. Although stereotypes are constructs in individual minds, the stereotypes of greatest interest to the study of social organization and interaction are those which are shared, i.e. *social* stereotypes. The critical questions for Tajfel concern the *functional* relationships between social stereotypes and the social groups that maintain them, and the processes whereby large numbers of people come to adopt the same (or similar) belief systems. As he puts it 'stereotypes can become *social* only when they are "shared" by large numbers of people within social groups or entities – the sharing implying a process of effective diffusion' (Tajfel 1981:145). The functional basis of sex role stereotypes is clearly related to the sex role stratification of society (though saying so scarcely explains the details of how the system works). The 'effective diffusion' of stereotypes is a question of obvious relevance to the present text and in beginning such an enquiry it is worth echoing Tajfel's implicit point that the study of the diffusion of ideas is critical to the study of the social order.

Sexism·

Although everybody forms stereotypes of at least some social groups (e.g. of shop assistants, professors, male chauvinists, policemen, Rastafarians, old people, members of the Conservative Party) and although we often find them useful in helping us to determine our behaviour towards other people, there are also liabilities attached to this way of systematizing the social environment. Because stereotypes are based upon generalizations, they can provide what Gergen and Gergen (1981:145) depict as a 'convenient quicksand', trapping us into biased and limited perceptions of individuals. This can lead to the attribution of properties purportedly associated with a group yet not necessarily shared by all (or even any) of its members, and can obscure actual properties of the unique individual we are assessing. The social psychological literature is replete with powerful demonstrations of the impact of ethnic, political and sexual stereotypes upon social judgements (see Deaux (1976), Eiser (1980), Tajfel (1981) and McArthur (1982) for examples and general discussions; the influence of sex role stereotypes on adults' perception of children will be discussed in Chapter 3).

Such limitations upon social perception are not of course merely structural–cognitive, but are often related to value judgements and affective dispositions towards the social category and its supposed characteristics: in short, they reflect the prejudices that different social groups engender towards each other (and towards themselves). Prejudice associated with sex role stereotypes is known by the relatively recent coinage 'sexism', and the term will be used in this book to denote unfavourable attitudes or actions towards a gender group and its members predicated solely or partly upon the basis of gender. Note that while sex role stereotypes and sexism may often be closely related in practice, they are not identical in principle. Thus, it is possible to hold a stereotyped view (for example, that most adult women are housewives) without endorsing what you might perceive as a negative state of affairs, and it is conceivable that an individual could acknowledge that there are no substantive psychological differences between the sexes, but still dislike a particular sex. This distinction between stereotyping and sexism will be of some relevance when we consider children's reactions to sex role stereotypes later in the book. Note too that sexism does not necessarily entail a thoroughgoing negativity towards a particular sex; self-evidently it is possible to be attracted to members of a sex on the basis of some criteria, but dislike them on others, or even to like them *because of* their perceived inferiority. Nevertheless, in general, stereotypes tend to be based upon *extreme* characteristics attributed to the stereotyped group, and human beings seem prone to attach values to extremes; quite often, these values are negative (McArthur 1982). Negative values about either sex constitute sexism.

Finally, it should be mentioned that in practice we will be concerned in this book with aspects of what is sometimes called *heterosexism*, that is, sexism within the context of male–female relations and within contexts which tend to assume that these are (prescriptively) normal. Although this excludes discussion of sex role matters relating to substantial minority groups (i.e. gay people), and therefore restricts the overall scope of the text, this unfortunate limitation reflects that fact that, as far as I am aware, no research has been undertaken to investigate the impact upon children of mass media portrayals of homosexual people. Similarly, child development researchers are generally unable to take methodological account of the fact that the eventual sexual preferences of any random sample of their subjects will be varied. One need only imagine the difficulties that would greet any researcher who attempted a study in this area to understand why this particular gap poses irresolvable problems that we just do not have the evidence to address here.

Later chapters will, therefore, be concerned with the possible consequences for young viewers, who are in the process of acquiring their sex roles, of watching sex role stereotypes in the course of their favourite everyday leisure activity. Before turning directly to this, it will be useful to review briefly some of the influential theories that form a backdrop to any study of mass media and audience.

Mass media research perspectives

Recurring issues in the history of mass media research include the question whether the media *reflect* society or *shape* it, and emphases of theorists diverge about the *sender–receiver* relationship, with some concentrating on the former, some the latter – and surprisingly few relating the two. It will not be possible here to give an exhaustive account of mass media theories (see Comstock *et al.* (1978), Withey and Abeles (1980), Howitt (1982) and McQuail (1983) for a range of recent discussions) and it is not entirely necessary to do so, since few of them have been exploited so far in the relatively recent growth of research into TV and sex roles. However, as will become clear in later chapters, researchers in this latter field have spent some time repeating the strategies of earlier media research, and of course many general concerns of mass communications researchers bear upon the specific topic of this book. For these reasons it will be useful to sketch out some of the main perspectives available.

Borrowing heavily from a particularly crisp outline provided by

Howitt (1982: Ch. 2), I will consider three models of mass communication research, namely the Cultural Ratification Model, the Effects Model, and the Uses and Gratification Model. I will also add a model which Howitt does not discuss, namely the Script Model. I will summarize the main points of each approach and then attempt to indicate the perspectives which each generates with respect to the particular topic of sex roles in television.

The cultural ratification model

Howitt (1982) describes this model as holding that the media act as agencies of political and ideological control, perpetuating images and world views compatible with the goals and preoccupations of the groups in power. The media are also seen by cultural ratification theorists as repressing contradictory and radical opinion. As Gross and Jeffries-Fox (1978:242) put it:

> Because media messages are commodities manufactured for sale, their perspective reflects institutional organization and control. The goal of greatest audience appeal at least cost demands that these messages follow conventional social morality.

With respect to sex role portrayals, this model would predict that conventional patterns will be represented, endorsed and exaggerated in the media. Certainly, as we will see in Chapter 2, there is plenty of evidence to support this much of the cultural ratification framework as applied to the specific topic of sex roles in television. However, the model also implies that cultural ratification has an effect, if not of instigating a social order at least of contributing to its perpetuation and continuation. This is where the model runs into difficulties. Howitt (1982:16) asserts that the empirical evidence in support of this approach is 'virtually non-existent', and is usually limited to analyses of media content. One problem is that the model recognizes that the media function among numerous potential agencies of the controlling powers in a society, and hence it is very difficult to detect the impact of what amounts to only part of a larger parcel. This is a broader issue to which we will return throughout the book, but note for the moment that it limits the predictive power of the model and also presents it with a cop-out when effects are not demonstrable.

Finally, note too that while the cultural ratification model has what may be an appealing ring of rhetoric which lends itself usefully to extension to account for the conspiratorial work of male, white middle-class agents of sexist oppression via the media, there must be a limit to the number of times we can discuss the fact that the world is inequitable (a descriptive achievement): far more challenging is to discover how the world works (an explanatory achievement). The cultural ratification model is important because of its emphasis on the functional relationship between media content and the social order, but limited because of its inability to specify causal dimensions unique to this transaction.

The effects model

The effects model is actually an umbrella term describing a variety of approaches that have in common an interest in the influence of the media upon the audience. The concern here is very much with how the world 'works', or at least those aspects of the social world in which the media may be substantially implicated. As Howitt remarks, 'effects' inquiries correspond essentially to public and political interests in the question 'just *what do the mass media do to people?*' (1982:7). Much of this book is concerned with how scientists have set about investigating the alleged effects of TV sex role portrayals upon children. Needless to say, the present author shares the belief of many other investigators that this is an important and research-worthy question; however, I agree too with Howitt that some precarious assumptions are often made in 'effects' approaches and that these stem in part from the metaphors that are employed in this approach to media research, and in part from quite unwarranted assumptions about the nature of the audience.

As Howitt points out, one conception of effects is the so-called 'hypodermic' model, according to which: 'the mass media *inject* into the audience a dose of persuasive communication which has a fairly uniform effect on the audience' (1982:7). Thus, in the present context, the viewer might be seen as receiving a daily treatment of sex role stereotypes which then influence his or her 'state of health' by causing the corresponding beliefs and attitudes to break out. A closely related conception, also discussed by Howitt, is the stimulus response (SR) or 'conditioning' model, borrowed from the learning theory paradigm of the early behaviourist psychologists. According to this model, the organism is exposed to a stimulus as a means of encouraging or extinguishing some response. Again, for present purposes, we might imagine the viewer receiving a repetitive positive reinforcement whereby traditionally sex stereotyped behaviours, such as shooting bad guys or looking like *Pam Ewing*, are 'rewarded' vicariously, in the first case by seeing bad guys fall over and being admired by beautiful women, in the second by gaining the attentions of powerful males and by joining the wealthy.

One concomitant of the effects approach has been usefully characterized by Williams (1981) as the 'linear effects' assumption, according to which the greater the viewer's exposure to the stimulus, the greater the effect – or as Williams puts it: 'the more people watch, the more they learn' (1981:182). This conception underlies much work on the 'effects' of TV and it has considerable appeal to lay thinking. In present terms, it suggests that the more sex stereotyped content a child views, the more traditional his or her own beliefs and attitudes will become. This assumption has been accepted by many commentators upon, and several investigators of, TV and sex role development and I will devote considerable space to a fuller examination of the arguments and evidence later in the book.

For the moment, it is worth stressing that there are substantial conceptual weaknesses in the kinds of effects models sketched here, as well as serious methodological hurdles before them. Some of the general issues are elaborated by Howitt (1982:9–11). In the present context, the main problems are (a) that the conception of 'the audience' in the effects approach is often severely limited, and (b) that, as noted in discussing the cultural ratification model, it is very difficult to disentangle the effects of the media, or a single medium, from those due to the myriad of other social forces conceivably impinging upon the developing individual. The limited conceptualization of the audience is something we can at least attempt to tackle by stressing at the outset that it includes everybody who watches TV. The audience is people of all ages, of both sexes, in all social classes, at all levels of intellect and social understanding, in diverse family or institutional structures, and with every conceivable value and belief system at various degrees of sophistication. Tackling this multiplicity in systematic research is really an obstacle to effects research rather than an inevitable theoretical weakness, but unfortunately it is the case that effects researchers tend to assume an homogeneous effect irrespective of audience characteristics. Thus, effects models often fail to address the mechanisms and processes supposedly occurring and to relate these to models of viewer understanding and, in the case of children, to developmental changes.

The uses and gratifications model

The uses and gratifications model takes a somewhat different perspective on the mass media by focusing on the functions that the media serve for the audience. Thus, attention in this approach is receiver- rather than sender-oriented. Theorists developing this model have provided typologies of the functions that audiences seek to gratify in their media. According to one school of thought (McQuail 1983: 82–83), these include *information, personal identity, integration* and *social interaction* and *entertainment*. Relating McQuail's model to sex roles, then, we might posit that a medium such as TV could be a convenient source of well-illustrated *information* about male and female behaviour. It could provide models and reinforcement for a sense of *personal (gender) identity*. It could allow us to check that our social beliefs and attitudes are compatible with the society in which we wish to be *integrated* and provide substitutes for real-life companionship by affording para-social interaction with the glamorous and powerful. Among TV's *entertainment* functions could be voyeuristic sexual gratification by virtue of vicarious involvement with attractive stars.

The advantages of this approach are that it takes account of the active potential of the media user to select, to attend, to value and to dismiss media content, and that it at least points the way towards a structured account of the complex transactions that we might suspect to exist between audience and media. The difficulties of the approach include the fact that, as McQuail (1983:164) points out, there is a lot of 'noise' in the communication system – by which he means that much media use is casual and routine, and hence it is difficult to identify exactly which elements of which bit of exposure are gratifying which 'need' of the user. Obviously, given the pervasiveness of TV, this problem is particularly pertinent in the case of the medium that concerns us here. Other problems, reviewed by Howitt (1982), are that it is difficult to define precisely what are the social and psychological needs that the media are supposedly gratifying and that the model says little about the origins of these needs.

The script model

This is the least developed of the mass communication theories discussed here. Indeed, it is a theory which is actually 'located' elsewhere, at the points of intersection among work in artificial intelligence, linguistics and social psychology (Schank and Abelson 1977) and has only quite recently been related to the mass media in speculative theoretical accounts (e.g. Withey 1980; Janis 1980; Roloff 1981). Hence, the reader should be warned that like most borrowed theories, current estimates of its promise may turn out to be inversely related to the amount of evidence available to test it. However, it is an attractive approach because it addresses phenomena, central to the nature of the mass media, which are curiously neglected by some of the traditional theories. These include the ways in which information, particularly information about social events, is structured in the media. Because this relates to issues in the study of how children structure information about social events and relations which we will address later in the book, it will be useful to consider briefly the main principles of the script approach.

Script theory is concerned essentially with how human beings organize information about sequences of action. As the title suggests, the basic proposition is that we attempt to understand the spatial and temporal world, and to plan our own behaviour within it, by constructing 'scripts'. A script is a generalized and hierarchically ordered event representation, typically organized towards a goal or set of goals.

A concrete example might be the 'tutorial script'. In a typical University tutorial, there are a limited number of persons enacting pre-established roles (e.g. lecturer, student) in an ordered way towards meeting some overall goal (e.g. to advance the student's learning). The sequence of events can be represented as a series of subscripts, based around the events of *arrival* (the student knocks at the door, enters, greetings are exchanged, etc.), *focus* (the lecturer guides the conversation to the academic subject of the meeting, the student produces some relevant material such as an essay, notes), *discussion* (an exchange of opinions the quality of which will be influenced by the personalities, moods, skills and preparation of the participants), *exit* (the discussion is terminated, arrangements for future meetings/workload are made, farewells uttered and the student leaves). Anybody who has participated in the rich interpersonal discourse of such an event sequence will recognize the scope for variation, digression and abandonment of the skeletal script presented here, but note that certain aspects of the structure are inevitable. For example, one cannot *exit* before *arrival*. This seems so obvious as to be trivial, but part of the interest of script theory is that it attempts to capture the regularities in and the constraints upon our social representations, and it proposes that these are far from trivial but actually provide valuable bases for predictability. To illustrate that these are non-trivial, consider a student who knows how to perform the discrete behaviours of saying 'Hello', of asking questions, and of making farewells – but has no grasp of the appropriate order of these activities, and engages in them in reverse. Jumbling the order of a routine social event can cause chaos; knowing the order makes it easier to understand the interdependence of events and the meaning of particular actions.

According to the script theorists, then, a script is a generalized representation which supports the process of understanding the streams of behaviour that we observe or participate in. Now the relevance of this model to the study of the mass media should be immediately obvious. Much of the entertainment media, certainly much of TV, is based upon stories, narratives and other forms of, quite literally, scripts. Furthermore, there is powerful intuitive evidence to suggest that as media users we learn from the repetitive scripts we view. For example, how else would you know precisely what to do when, while leading a chain of wagons through hostile Injun territories, you detect approaching war cries? How else would we all get so many opportunities to be first years at Oxford, Cambridge, Harvard and Yale, to lunch with *Krystle Carrington*, to win the Second World War, and to pillage Saxon hamlets? These social skills have been scripted for us many times, and we all know quite a lot about the roles, the goals, and the event sequences that they entail.

Returning to the specific topic of sex roles, it is obvious that these figure regularly in some of the most popular of media scripts: especially love stories and family histories. We began the chapter with a couple of examples of fragments of the sexual script, and any viewer knows that the popular media reiterate and embellish these very frequently (Roloff 1981).

Some of the attractions of taking a script approach to understanding the media have been outlined perceptively by Withey (1980), and they include the advantage that by interpreting the elements of a communication with reference to a structured account of their context, we gain a better characterization of their (potential) meaning. For example, on a check list of televised incidents, a man buying a woman a cocktail might be recorded as an act of chivalry, a preliminary to seduction, or a symbol of sexist patronage. But if the man is *J.R.* and the woman is *Sue Ellen*, then any educated person would recognize instantly that he is trying to set her once more on the slippery slope to alcohol abuse. To understand his motives we would need to know something of the general script into which these figures are locked (i.e. what's been going on between them over the years), and to understand his strategy we would need to know something of the specific script governing that particular strand of that particular episode (e.g. has *Sue Ellen* been under some especial stress lately which it suits *J.R.* to exploit with this temptation?). Only by reference to our knowledge of the intricate interweaving of event sequences around the *Southfork* household could we hope to detect the full subtleties of this manoeuvre. The fact that we may be equipped to do so easily should not be taken as a sign that these are uninteresting processes. Even viewing a soap opera calls upon quite complex underlying cognitive organization.

A second important feature of the script model is that it offers a more potent metaphor of the viewer's use of information. As Withey (1980:14) puts it: 'One develops a kind of repertoire for dealing with aspects of the world. A repertoire is a more complex idea than an attitude.' Human beings do seem to have repertoires for dealing with aspects of their world, and script (and related schema) models are currently providing useful reference points for social psychologists attempting to understand how they do so (Abelson 1976). What makes the model particularly interesting in relation to the mass media is that here we are (or could be) centrally concerned with the meshing of scripts – the sender's and the receiver's. For successful communication, the sender has to achieve a recognizable script and has to make correct guesses about what can be presupposed (i.e. how much the viewer knows and understands), while the receiver has to be able to discover what the script is, and what is central and what is peripheral. Thus questions arise such as: do we acquire scripts from TV? Do we interpret TV in frameworks dictated by our existing scripts? Do these processes interact?

Although this model has not been worked out and tested in detail in mass media research, it has the appeal that it creates an explanatory perspective from which to investigate both medium and user, a perspective which directs attention to critical aspects of the organization of television information and to the organizational commitments of the active viewer; it is thus interactional and dynamic. Finally, its particular relevance in the present context reflects the fact that roles, after all, are things enacted in scripts.

Although we have not exhausted here the variety of theories available which attempt to account for mass media influences, this brief survey indicates something of the diversity of perspectives that can be taken. It indicates too the difficulties of ascertaining precisely how something as complex as a mass medium relates to something even more complex, such as a society composed of millions of people. In fact, we have only considered part of the equation here, and defer until Chapter 3 discussion of theories of social development that also bear directly upon the topic of sex roles. First, we need to consider the 'message', that is the images of sex roles that television presents, and we turn to this in the next chapter.

TWO

First the bad news: the sex role content of television

> The superiority of the male is indeed overwhelming: Perseus, Hercules, David, Achilles, Lancelot, the old French warriors Du Geslin and Bayard, Napoleon – so many men for one Joan of Arc.
> (de Beauvoir 1949:30)

As I have already suggested in the Introduction, it is not difficult to find examples of sex role stereotypes in television. You do not need to be a social scientist to discern some of the underlying patterns in everyday representations of the sexes on our screens, and of course many people, both inside and outside of the broadcasting industry, have criticized this pervasive aspect of television. The evidence we can collect simply by switching on our sets may well be sufficient for many people's purposes, whether it be to fuel wrath at the wanton sexism perpetuated in the mass media or to confirm a belief that things are pretty much as they should be.

However, from the social scientist's perspective, there are limits to the value of impressionistic data such as might be gleaned from casual observation. If we wish to develop adequate descriptions of this aspect of the social world, and in turn to advance explanatory theories of the possible effects – and even of how to bring about meaningful change – then we need some more systematic approach to the analysis of sex role content in television. Just how pervasive is stereotyping? What forms does it take, what values does it maintain? How enduring is it in the face of well over a decade of widespread public debate over sex role allocation?

In fact, social scientists of various disciplines have addressed these and related questions in numerous studies conducted over the last 15 years or so. This chapter presents a review of some of the main findings. The overall result of these investigations is indeed to confirm that television presents highly stereotyped and distorted images of the status and behaviour of males and females. But the work does much more than discover the obvious. It provides quantitative information on the frequency of certain stereotypical portrayals, and exposes subtleties in the representation of the sexes that may not be immediately transparent even to the critical viewer. It also contributes towards a qualitative account of how sex role stereotypes are structured and, importantly, helps us to construct a picture of the kind of information that forms part of the potential input to children learning about the social world.

Content analysis: the method

Most of the findings to be summarized in the following were obtained by researchers exploiting techniques of content analysis, a widely used method for quantifying 'the manifest content of communication' (Berelson 1952). A typical content analysis is conducted by first choosing an area of content in a medium (e.g. race relations, political news, sex roles) and constructing a categorical framework in which units of analysis can be defined reasonably specifically (e.g. abusive racial comments, mentioning an opposition party, males *vs*. female appearance, etc.) and then scoring the relative frequency of occurrence of these items within samples of medium output.

Although the technique is a popular one, it has serious limitations. There is often a strong element of subjective impression involved in the scoring process: for example, not everyone would agree on what constitutes an abusive racial comment, and even the same words may mean different things when uttered by different people (for instance, the term 'nigger' spoken by a white policeman or by a black radical). To some extent, these problems can be met by explicit definition of scoring criteria, which at least then make the 'raw data' available to alternative interpretations. Another safeguard is to have more than one scorer analyse (independently) the same content, and check the correspondence between analyses (statistical reliability). This sounds quite respectable but even this runs into the problem that once the scorers have been trained in the application of a particular set of criteria, the investigator could be testing little more than their abilities to enforce his or her theoretical biases.

This is a particularly delicate problem in the present context, where many content analyses of sex role stereotypes in the mass media have been conducted by researchers avowedly committed to feminist perspectives. It is conceivable that when scoring a phenomenon such as 'male dominance', feminists display greater perspicacity in discovering such elements in human interactions than might less socially aware coders, or that they may interpret as symbols of male oppression incidents which others would interpret differently. A reliability check in such an investigation might tell us something about the extent to which two or more collaborating feminist researchers agree with each other, but the interpretation of their claims may still be open.

There are yet more fundamental problems with content analyses in terms of their ability to capture the social *meaning* of the data they address, and of the gaps they leave. We will return to these problems later in the chapter. However, despite this sceptical preamble, it should be said that there are still very good grounds for taking note of what content analyses of sex roles in television tell us. First, notwithstanding any reservations we may have about reliability and validity within individual studies, congruent findings across several investigations do begin to uncover patterns that it would be perverse to ignore: in fact, some of the data to be discussed shortly are so stark and so consistent that questions of reliability amount to little more than nitpicking. Secondly, as Butler and Paisley (1980:60) point out in a defence of this methodology, a creative analysis can direct our attention to subtle phenomena that might not be readily apparent to the lay observer, and thus uncover elements in the medium that enable us to construct a better model of its overall structure. We will see several examples of such analyses in the following. Thirdly, it has to be said that, at present, content analyses are the most prolific feature of research output in this field. Lots of them have been undertaken but few alternatives have been attempted: they form an inevitable starting point.

Content analysis: the findings

Television programmes can be classified in various ways, but for the purposes of organizing the large number of relevant studies available, I will divide them simply into programmes intended for adults, and programmes intended for children. In fact children watch much more than that ostensibly designated for them, either because older members of the family are viewing other programmes, or through personal preference developing during middle childhood (see Comstock *et al.* 1978:183f.). It is important, therefore, to.look at the findings for all areas of television, and as we will see in the following, the patterns tend to be quite similar in most types of material.

Sex role stereotyping in adult's television

One of the bluntest findings to emerge from study after study is that males appear much more frequently in television than females. Butler and Paisley (1980) reviewed 13 studies of the relative frequencies of appearance of men and women in television programmes and report that, overall, 72% of the characters were male, 28% were female. Now for some of the behavioural characteristics we will be considering shortly, detectable sex differences in the portrayals are at least open to the defence that males and females *do* differ to some degree on these dimensions. In fact, this turns out to be a weak defence, but it is worth noting that it does not bear much credence at all when we consider the demographic issues raised here: patently, in the real world males do not outnumber females by a ratio of 7:3. In most societies, women actually outnumber men. In terms of head counts, television's version of the male–female distribution is clearly at odds with the world around us, and the consistent reports of this bias produced by numerous content analyses cannot reasonably be accounted for in terms of any feminist bias in the investigators. But it can be accounted for in terms of sexist bias in the medium.

When we examine the status and activities of the men and women on our screens, further differences emerge. For example, Dominick (1979) investigated the percentages of (US) television programmes shown during peak viewing hours (prime-time) that had only men or only women in starring roles. Dominick's study was extensive, covering 1314 programmes shown during the years 1953–1977. He found that shows *exclusively* starring women never comprised more than 14% of prime-time programmes in any season, and in many years the percentage was well below even this figure. Programmes exclusively starring males, on the other hand, accounted on average for about 45% of prime-time programmes. Over the whole 25-year period he investigated, Dominick found that females occupied starring roles only about 30% of the time (i.e. taking into account programmes not exclusively starring a single sex). For every *Cagney and Lacey* there is not only a *Starsky and Hutch* but also a *Magnum, Hannibal Smith, Columbo, Petrocelli, Ironside, McCloud, Rockford, T. J. Hooker, Crockett and Tubbs, Serpico* and *Kojak*.

So there is clear evidence that there is a numerical imbalance in the appearances of males and females in much of adult television, and that women are substantially less likely to be given the major, starring roles. The next question that has interested researchers is: what kinds of occupational and social roles do males and females have in television?

Investigations concerned with this issue have revealed that males are more often portrayed in employment than females (De Fleur 1964) and more males are shown in higher status occupations than females (Seggar and Wheeler 1973: Downing 1974; Tedesco 1974). The kinds of jobs in which women are employed in the world of television tend to be limited to those occupations traditionally viewed as female, such as secretary and nurse (Seggar and Wheeler 1973; Kaniuga *et al.* 1974). Seggar and Wheeler (1973) compared their data on TV content with US census data and found that portrayals of both sexes clashed with the realities of occupational distribution: in both sexes professional and technical workers were over-represented.

It is not surprising to find that substantial proportions of women characters are represented as housewives (Butler and Paisley 1980; Long and Simon 1974). It has also been found that the marital status of women is revealed more often than that of men (Tedesco 1974; Downing 1974; McNeil 1975) and that female characters are usually younger than males (Downing 1974). The majority of women shown in television appear to be aged under 30, according to a study conducted by Aronoff (1974). It seems reasonable to suppose that the disproportionate emphasis on women in this age group is closely connected to the representation of many females in television as sex objects (Butler and Paisley 1980; Durkin 1985a). Men, on the other hand, are often shown in positions of economic and social power, and it is consistent with this high status to be older than, but still enjoy the company of, the decorative females around. One manifestation of this is in commercials, where advertisers seem to prefer older men or younger women to sell their products. Harris and Feinberg (1977) suggest that older men are often used as high status authority figures in ads, whereas females lose value with age as far as selling products goes. *Telly Savalas* may be a commanding figure when extolling the virtues of *Bacardi Rum* but the likelihood of finding women of the same age group, same weight-to-height ratio, and same hairstyle lolling on his arms in his Caribbean playground while he sells it is, frankly, slight.

In an interesting study, Manes and Melnyk (1974) analysed the marital status of television females according to their level of occupational achievement. Compared with male job holders, employed females were depicted as less likely to be married, less likely to be *successfully* married, and more likely to be unsuccessfully married. The figures are striking: married women who held jobs were ten times more likely to be shown as unsuccessful in marriage than were housewives. As we have seen from the studies above, women are less likely in general to be shown in employment and in positions of high attainment; Manes and Melnyk's investigation reveals that where women *are* seen as achieving some level of occupational status, then this is likely to be associated with unsuccessful or unhappy personal lives.

How do the sexes interact on television? Generally, males are represented as more dominant than females (Turow 1974; Lemon 1977, 1978), and women are commonly shown acting in deference to their husbands (Long and Simon 1974) or as subordinates and adjuncts to men (Hennessee and Nicholson 1972; Manstead and McCulloch 1981). There is more likely to be a *MacMillan and Wife* than a *Rhoda and Husband*. Generally, both sexes are shown as fairly intelligent in television, but males are shown as more so (Busby 1975): *Jennifer Hart* is sophisticated, articulate and beautiful, but *Jonathan Hart* is generally that bit brighter and always in charge. The difference in intellect is most marked in ads, where females are often portrayed as unintelligent, in contrast to the male sources of scientific or factual information relating to the qualities of the product (Hennessee and Nicholson 1972).

Perhaps the most striking of all the figures here are those for the proportions of males and females who provide the 'voiceovers' in ads. Voiceovers usually contain the authoritative recommendations of the commercials, and several studies have found that men are much more likely to be used for this task. In one recent British ad for kitchen furnishings, for example, *Ms Felicity Kendall* served to demonstrate how the doors open and what the cupboards hold, but she was so manifestly impressed at the ingenuities of the manufacturers that she was unable to complete any sentence describing the objects, and had to rely on gushing and oohing to convey her sentiments. Meanwhile, the genial voice of *Mr Terry Wogan* took command of the scenario and helped the viewer to strike a balance between feminine enthusiasm and masculine knowledgeability. Males, in fact, account for between 84% and 94% of voiceovers (Dominick and Rauch 1972; Pyke and Stewart 1974; Culley and Bennett 1976; Maracek *et al.* 1978; Manstead and McCulloch 1981). The reader can check this for him or herself: there really are very few ads in which a female voice commands you to buy, invites you to tell the difference between margarine and butter, or tries to persuade you that you'll be a better householder when you fit double-glazing. Thus, not only are between-sex interactions within television constrained, but television seems ill disposed to try to influence the viewer via a female agent.

Sex role stereotyping in children's television

Television material designated for children reaches a very high proportion of its intended audience (BBC 1974; Comstock *et al.* 1978).

It is then of particular interest to a developmental account of the possible influence of television in sex role acquisition to consider what content analyses of this area of the medium tell us about the representation of males and females. There are several such studies and their findings generally fit in with those established in the investigations of adult programming just described.

Once again, we find a numerical imbalance between the sexes, and it is sometimes even more marked than that found in adult television. Examination of recent offerings in children's TV in Britain, for example, reveals many programmes in which males are the main or sole stars: *Knight Rider, Fonz and the Happy Days Gang, Dr Who, Star Trek, The Little Green Man, He-Men and the Masters of the Universe* and *Dastardly and Muttley*. Generally, 70–85% of visible characters in children's television are male (Poulos *et al.* 1976; Busby 1975; O'Kelly 1974; Barcus 1977; Nolan *et al.* 1977). Levinson (1973) found that this distribution obtained in children's cartoon programmes both when human characters were represented, and when 'animals' starred. As far as I know, the animal kingdom affords proportions of males to females comparable to the ratio in humans, but this is scarcely reflected in the hormone balance of the stars of *Tom and Jerry, The Puppy's New Adventures, Basil Brush, Roland Rat* and *Scooby, Scrappy and Yabba Doo*.

Dohrmann (1975) found that, in US educational programmes, males comprised 100% of the leading characters, a result even starker than Dominick's (1979) survey of male–female stars in adult television, discussed above. Similarly, McArthur and Eisen (1976) compared the proportion of male to female figures in advertisements for children with those for adults (analysed in McArthur and Resko 1975). The adult figures were 57% males *vs.* 43% females; in children's ads the ratio was 80% to 20%. In fact, in order to find material to conduct a comparison of male and female characters for their study, Sternglanz and Serbin (1974) had to discard half of the most popular children's programmes then showing on US television because they contained no females at all! When females are shown in occupational roles in children's TV, they occupy a very narrowly defined range in contrast to males (Levinson 1973).

Studies of the behaviour of male and female characters in children's television reveal some differences, though the overall picture is not clear or consistent (see Durkin (1985a) for a fuller discussion). Sternglanz and Serbin (1974), for example, in a careful analysis found that males were significantly more likely to be shown as aggressive, constructive and succourant, while females were more likely to be shown as deferent. These findings are broadly in line with the patterns found in adult programmes. On the other hand, these investigators found no sex differences when characters were rated for *activity*, *dominance, autonomy, harm avoidance, nurturance, recognition* and *self recognition*. Further, another well designed study by McArthur and Eisen (1976) found no significant differences in rates of aggression of male and female characters (although the means tended towards the expected difference). McArthur and Eisen did find that males were more active *per se* in the programmes they analysed, and that *proportionately*, males engaged in slightly more aggressive behaviour than females. Dohrmann (1975) found that males were responsible for a clear majority of 'active masterly behaviour' in the educational programmes she studied, and that males were responsible for 100% of physical aggressions, and 94% of verbal aggressions.

There is, then, some lack of consistency in the studies of children's television. This may in part be due to different coding criteria used by different researchers, but it may also be due to changes over time and across networks in the types of programmes shown. Since the late 1960s, for example, there has been a great deal of public concern about violence in children's television and this may have affected some aspects of some channels' content, and thus have led to variations in the results of studies carried out in the early 1970s.

Nevertheless, when we look carefully, subtle but intriguing differences still stand out: an example of this is a study by Welch *et al.* (1979). These researchers examined the *form* of children's commercials, analysing the pace, amount of action, visual and auditory techniques of ads directed at boys and girls respectively, as well as commercials intended for children of either sex. They found marked differences according to the sex of the intended market. Ads selling boys' toys showed the products involved in more activity than was found in either of the other types of ads. Commercials directed at girls had more 'fades' and 'dissolves', and were accompanied by more soft background music. The sound effects in the boys' ads tended to be loud and dramatic. As Welch *et al.* (1979) point out, it is not just the content of children's advertisements which present different frequencies of males and females and portray stereotyped behaviour, but the forms and style of the commercials are also offering different emphases seemingly oriented around gender lines.

Some remaining questions

The content analyses tell us quite a lot about the differential treatment of the sexes in TV, but there are some gaps left by this mode of investigation and many questions remain for future investigation. The main problem is that content analyses concentrate primarily upon the *counting* of instances of given phenomena rather than upon exposing the *organization* of these elements. Thus, they reflect sex role stereotypes in the medium mainly at the level of traits (see Chapter 1) and of relatively discrete behaviours. They offer only gross character-izations of the *meaning* of the content, even within the terms of the individual programmes assessed. The significance of a particular behavioural act may be lost or misrepresented in this way, and the importance of a unifying structure may be ignored. The interrela-tionship of whole sequences of events, which is often critical to the nature and interpretation of textual information such as TV material, is left unexamined by content analysis. Intuitively, it seems obvious to us as viewers that TV regularly packages and presents images in ways intended to endorse certain value systems and exclude others, but how values are integrated around these 'bits' of sex role stereotypes, and how the dynamics of their interrelationships are conveyed, are neglected issues.

In short, we lack an account of the scripts (see Chapter 1), surface and underlying, in which sex role portrayals in TV are located, and in the absence of such an account the description of the raw data that the medium transmits is incomplete. There is actually a risk that content analyses alone may draw too simple a picture, generating a straight-forward dichotomy whereby males and females are perceived as radically different with an unambiguous dominance relationship. Among other drawbacks, this oversimplification minimizes attention to *within*-sex treatments in TV, and overlooks matters such as the interaction of sex with class and race. Such a state of affairs may be adequate for polemical purposes in public debate – it is not too difficult to confirm that TV is sexist – but it is a handicap to scientific research into the possible effects of the material not to have a more penetrating account of how it is structured.

There are, then, limitations to our present account of TV sex role content that call for more investigations using a more diverse range of methodologies. However, it would be perverse to ignore the strong evidence of bias that any method from content analysis to casual viewing exposes, and we need not wait for an exhaustive treatment before wondering what contribution all of this makes to the world in which children grow up.

Are things changing?

Since the early 1970s, sex roles have been the focus of considerable public attention. Much of the interest has been aroused by various women's movements and these have led to widespread questioning of traditional role allocations especially, but not only, among the white middle-class of North America and Europe. For a variety of reasons, including the vociferousness of the pressure groups concerned and the privileged access of the middle-classes to posts in the media industry, we might expect the mass media to have begun to react to developments in the society around them. Groups such as *Women in Media* have lobbied for more equitable treatment of females in TV, and several writers have offered guidelines and recommendations to assist those willing in the media to combat sexism (Butler and Paisley 1980; Whipple and Courtney 1980), as well as pointing out that sexism in TV representations may be flouting equal rights legislation in at least some countries (Axelrad 1976). What signs are there, then, that television is moderating its hitherto distorted treatment of sex roles?

It is worth stressing that most of the findings we have been considering so far are concerned with patterns and balance rather than with absolutes. Taking the issue of the sex ratio, for example, there are, and have been since the early days of the medium, *some* women in starring roles. Most readers can probably think of some contemporary television characters who provide exceptions: *Cagney & Lacey*, *Charlie's Angels*, *WonderWoman* are recent examples, but, as we have seen, the statistics suggest that they remain exceptions. It is also obviously the case that not all of these women are free from sex-object status.

But are there changes in the behavioural patterns of today's male and female television characters? There is not a great deal of hard evidence available, but the few studies that have been addressed to this question do not indicate radical developments. While we can think of occasional female stars, and females on television who are more active and assertive than the core feminine stereotype would promote, it is more difficult to find male characters who are cast substantially apart from stereotypes.

Downs (1981) compared male and female television characters on 11 behavioural categories derived from a list of widely held beliefs about sex differences. He found significant differences on only three: *work orientation* (men were more likely than women to be shown performing occupational-related duties), *home orientation* (women were more often shown in the home) and *emotionality* (women were more likely to express upset or to cry). These are of course in line with traditional stereotyping. No differences were found, though, on the categories *high sociability*, *low sociability*, *verbal aggression*, *assertiveness*, *confidence*, *empathy* and *fearfulness*. Downs suggests that it is possible that sex role stereotyping is diminishing. However, as we have seen elsewhere in this chapter, some variation across studies may be expected due to differences in scoring criteria. It would have been interesting to have seen the results of a comparison between, say, programmes of 1970 and programmes of 1980, using Downs's categories. This would be a stronger basis upon which to evaluate claims of changes. Downs did find also that males were more likely to solve their own problems, while females were more likely to deal with the problems of others or to seek help in tackling their own. This study does reveal that stereotyping is not always so rigid that every measure an investigator employs is likely to produce a significant between-sex difference.

Weigel and Loomis (1981), for example, attempted to replicate Manes and Melnyk's (1974) study, discussed on p. 26, in which television was shown to present work and marriage as incompatible commitments for women. Manes and Melnyk had collected their data in 1972, and Weigel and Loomis in 1978. Weigel and Loomis found, consistent with Manes and Melnyk, that female job holders were more likely than males to be unmarried. There was *some* indication of change, though in that Weigel and Loomis found no difference among married male and female job holders in terms of the *success* of their marriage.

It seems reasonable to agree with Weigel and Loomis that some progress may have come about during the 1970s, although it has to be added that the causes and correlates of the changes are not clear. A cynical view might be that television is moving towards a new male chauvinistic awareness, that it can be in a man's financial interests to have his wife go out to work, and consequently such a development is no longer represented as so disharmonious as in recent times. From a slightly different perspective, it could be argued that television is reflecting an increasing pattern in Western families to depend on a 'second income' as an essential component of the family budget, and again this economic adjustment may be prompting some role accommodation. Finally, it is worth adding that Weigel and Loomis did not report any increase in the frequency of males experiencing the strain between their domestic (say, child care) responsibilities and their occupations. Stereotypical male arrangements remain the standard against which to check progress in the status and treatment of females, at least in the occupational domain.

Kalisch *et al.* (1981) have examined changes in film portrayals of members of a traditionally female occupation, nursing, from the 1930s to the 1970s. The findings reveal a shift during the 1970s away from traditionally nurturant, maternal, self-sacrificing and patriotic images, with nurses increasingly portrayed in recent films as hostile, sadistic and promiscuous. These findings are interesting, but could be interpreted in different ways. On the one hand, they may reflect a departure from unrealistically gentle and servile pictures of female health care workers, while on the other hand, they may signify some movement towards an increasingly negative representation of a largely female occupation. It is difficult to evaluate these possibilities out of context (without reference to the scripts in which they occur) and the explanation may be more complex. For example, it is probably true to say that in recent years more socially-aware and critical films have been produced in which institutions such as hospitals and mental health establishments have come under scrutiny. Thus, some of the nurses in *One Flew Over the Cuckoo's Nest* may count as sadistic females in a content analysis, but (one might surmise) the purpose of the film was to draw attention to the processes within a mental health hospital, an institution which would typically have some female staff, rather than to demean women *per se*. Similarly, the demise of 'patriotism' in nurses which Kalisch *et al.* found could be due to decreasing numbers of glorifying films about war. After all, for some social theorists patriotism is the last refuge of the scoundrel.

Among other recent studies, Manstead and McCulloch (1981) found ample evidence of stereotyping in British television commercials, and Knill *et al.* (1981) found that US television commercials broadcast in 1980 appeared to be much the same in terms of their treatments of male and female roles as the patterns reported in earlier studies. One change which Knill *et al.* did record was that women appeared to be being given more powerful roles as product representatives and consumers, especially in afternoon advertisements.

As pointed out earlier, women aged over 30 are not in abundance in TV generally and in commercials particularly. When they do appear they tend to be presented engaged in domestic chores, as traditional mother figures or as Mrs Mops. One exception to this pattern appeared on British and other European screens in 1984, when 'a rather ravishing and immaculately turned-out 44 year old' (Gable 1984) was used to sell a new shampoo, *Empathy*, marketed at the over 40s. The manufacturers, Johnson and Johnson, had learned that some 13 million British women were aged over 40, and promptly invented a shampoo with 'secret ingredients' that met the particular requirements of hair in this age bracket. The theme of the resulting TV ads was that it is quite an achievement for a woman aged over 40 to make herself eye catching, but regular application of *Empathy* shampoo should do the trick. The fact that the appearance in a commercial of a woman who was both over 40 and 'rather ravishing' evoked a *Sunday Times* article, revealing the further claim that 'Women are writing in to thank us for the product and for acknowledging their specific needs' (Jacqueline Stevenson, 25, an agency representative, quoted in Gable, 1984), is itself a sign of the rarity of such a representation on our television screens.

One area of genuine change over the past ten years or so has been the increasing use of women as newsreaders. This role was once virtually exclusively male, apparently because TV directors believed the audience would find it difficult to take female newsreaders seriously as authoritative sources (Stone 1972). With the decision makers nursing such convictions, it is perhaps understandable why one early female newsreader in Chicago was presented, according to Eddings (1980), delivering the evening news from the heart-shaped bed of the programme's sponsor! It is now quite common to find women newsreaders on all television channels, and they usually sit at the desk. While several women have become national and international TV 'personalities' through this role, the development is not an unqualified breakthrough, as it has been objected that women are still restricted in terms of the types of field reporting they are allocated (Eddings 1980). It could also be complained that female newsreaders are more likely to be selected for their physical attractiveness than are males, though it is difficult to determine to what extent self-selection operates here (i.e. attractive women may be more inclined to apply for highly visible posts).

Most of the accounts of changes have been concerned with adult television. I am unaware of any recent content analysis of the sex role content of children's television and it is possible that more substantial changes have come about in this area of broadcasting than elsewhere. Certainly, unsystematic inspection of British children's television gives the impression that more women can be found here in central roles than elsewhere on television, and there appear to be some presenters and characters in entertainment for children who are not heavily sex typed. Even so, as noted earlier, there remain many exclusively or predominantly male programmes in this area of broadcasting. While relevant quantitative investigations would be useful, it should be borne in mind that, as noted at the beginning of the chapter, children watch much more television than that which the television companies produce specifically for them.

Overall, it seems that there are some noteworthy but not extensive changes occurring in the contemporary mass media. The pattern of development tends to be consistent with the directions exhorted by some women's groups: women are entering some previously male preserves, such as newsreading. But elsewhere on television it remains easy to find women still in a numerical minority, and still represented in traditional and stereotyped roles. The male sex role on television has received less direct attention, but in so far as many investigators take it as the obvious contrast to the female role, the data on differences suggest that the male role is presented in predominantly traditional ways and that there is little evidence of change in recent broadcasting. In sum, it seems that there is ample opportunity for the young viewer to find stereotyped, and often sexist, representations of male and female roles in television content. Which brings us to an important question to ask of any body of research findings: so what?

So what?

All of the analyses and observations reviewed in this chapter have been concerned with the *content* of television with respect to a particular domain of human social organization. The work is incomplete and inadequate in some ways, but nevertheless it reflects a rather large and productive investment of energy by numerous social scientists around the world and it contributes a reasonably informative picture of some of the social representations contained in our primary mass medium. Having acquired such information, we should now ask what it contributes to our understanding of the world around us.

Surprisingly, many commentators assume that the contribution is obvious: the content analyses tell us that much of television is reprehensible, and that it is likely to have a deleterious effect upon the young. In fact, two issues are conflated here, one ideological and the other psychological. Our assessment of the *desirability* of sex stereotyping in TV is a matter of value judgement, and presumably varies as a function of an individual's general perspective on human affairs. Our assessment of the *effects* of sex stereotyping in TV is, however, an empirical judgement, which should ideally be based upon an understanding of how human beings acquire social roles, and upon evidence of how a mass medium might contribute to these processes. Since television first became available, critics from numerous perspectives have readily assumed that it has a bad influence upon children. This may or may not be the case, but for the moment it should be stressed that no amount of content analyses can establish the correctness of such a view. They tell us the 'bad news', but it remains to be seen what are the consequences of the messages they uncover. To begin to consider this issue, we need first to address the more general question of how children acquire sex roles, and we turn to some accounts of this in the following chapter.

THREE

Theories of sex role acquisition

How do individual human beings come to adopt the patterns of appearance, behaviour, even of thought, that are expected within their societies to be associated with biological sex? A general account of these processes would clearly provide a valuable framework within which to examine the consequences of exposure to one possible variable, namely sex role stereotyping in television. In this chapter, I will outline some of the main theoretical approaches to the topic of sex role development and provide a brief review of the kinds of arguments and evidence that each calls upon. The chapter will not present an exhaustive account, because that would require a great deal more space than is available here, nor will it provide a conclusive account, because the topic is so complex that we do not yet have one. The main purposes of the chapter are to alert the reader unfamiliar with this field to the chief issues at stake and to place the specific treatment of television 'effects' which follows in a context which acknowledges the immensity of the explanatory task. To these ends, I will present summary discussions of three influential theoretical orientations and will attempt to specify in each case the predictions that it makes, explicitly or implicitly, about the possible contribution of television to sex role development.

The three main theoretical perspectives I will discuss are the biological, the environmental, and the cognitive-developmental. There are other approaches, but these three serve our purposes here by illustrating the chief emphases that guide most contemporary work. The first two of these are the scientific correlates of the most common lay views on sex roles: 'it's all biological' versus 'it's all learned'. I stress, though, that all these are lay opinions and, while they capture the reality that these two approaches do indeed differ radically on the nature–nurture issue, few exponents of the theories are actually quite as absolute as these slogans. The third theory, cognitive-developmental, is probably the dominant framework among developmental psychologists but perhaps the least familiar to lay persons or to students of other disciplines. This approach proposes that the child is a constructive agent who 'builds' his or her understanding of the physical and social world in accord with general organizational principles of cognitive development. I will discuss this third theory at greater length because I believe it provides a more adequate starting point than either of the others, but I will also outline some problems with this perspective that call for more careful attention to the *social* nature of role development, and I will discuss how a social dimension might be incorporated into the developmental study of sex roles.

Biological approaches

By definition, the sexes differ biologically. Initial classification by sex is based upon the possession of external physical attributes, most notably genitalia. These properties are the outcome of a biological process begun at conception, when the father contributes either an X chromosome which will unite with the mother's X chromosome, leading to the birth of a daughter, or a Y chromosome, leading to the birth of a son. The stages of physical development from the moment of conception onwards are reasonably well understood, and more detailed accounts can be found elsewhere (Money and Ehrhardt 1972; Brooks-Gunn and Matthews 1979; Archer and Lloyd 1982). The contentious issue, of course, is whether the biological facts can be shown to predetermine sex differences in behaviour from childhood onwards.

Researchers interested in these questions have focused on a variety of issues, but a central concern has been the effects of the hormone *testosterone* which, in the presence of the Y chromosome, is produced in greater amounts in male infants from about the sixth week of gestation. This stimulates the development of the male anatomy and predetermines an *acyclic* release of sex hormones beyond puberty. Considerable controversy exists over whether differential amounts of testosterone underlie behavioural differences between the sexes from childhood. Some biological theorists argue that greater amounts of male hormones may affect neural regulation and the expression of behaviour (cf. Hamburg and Lunde 1966), better equipping boys for physical activity and disposing them from infancy to engage vigorously in it (Hutt 1978). It has also been argued that the Y chromosome elicits more information from the genetic blueprint (Ounsted and Taylor 1972; Hutt 1978) with the consequence that maturation of the male is slower, allowing for greater phenotypic variation because of the greater possibilities for more biological potential to be expressed.

Space does not permit a full evaluation of these arguments and their correlates. It is sufficient to note that there are theories that attempt to explain supposed behavioural differences between the sexes in terms of biological differences. It will be useful, however, to look in slightly greater detail at one particular biological theory which attempts to provide a more comprehensive account of the organiz- ation of sex roles in societal structures, namely the sociobiological approach.

Sociobiologists maintain that a species' social behaviour is largely determined by biological endowment, which in turn is the outcome of evolutionary adaptation. This is held to be as true of humans as it is of the lower species. Hence, sociobiologists maintain that there is a sound biological explanation of behavioural differences between the sexes and the explanation begins in primeval times when the male's natural role evolved as that of the hunter and the female's became that of the child minder. The importance of male physiological advant- age and of the female role in reproduction to such an account is obvious.

Wilson (1975, 1978) is one of the most influential sociobiologists and, although much of his writing is devoted to animal behaviour, he has outlined how the evolutionary system has promoted sex differ- ences in humans. He holds that the nuclear family is the building block of human societies and that the family is the societal repercus- sion of the biological drives and tensions arising from evolutionary adaptation. Briefly, the argument is that because of the acyclic nature of the male's hormonal system (i.e. the fact that a male produces continuously millions of sperm) and the biologically-given motive to ensure survival of one's own genes, it is in the male's interest to procreate freely whenever the opportunity arises. The female, how- ever, produces only one egg at a time and each pregnancy constrains her behaviour for quite lengthy periods, normally followed by even lengthier child-rearing responsibilities. It is in her interests, therefore, not to procreate freely, but instead to ensure that she bestows her favours only when she is assured of enduring support and allegiance from a protective male. Simply put, the female needs to know that, if she is going to be stuck in the cave for several months, then her devoted male will be out hunting for food rather than off indulging his procreative drives elsewhere.

How do humans resolve this seeming incompatibility of sexual goals? According to some sociobiologists, the family has evolved as the institutionalized compromise. While the male has the advantage of unlimited sperm, the female has the advantage that she can be sure that any child she bears is hers, and that it therefore perpetuates her genes. So while there are factors motivating the female to ensnare a male protector there are equally good reasons for the male, who wants to be sure he is raising his own genes, to secure his female from the attentions of other males. Thus, the female has developed forms of behaviour intended to enhance her sexual appeal and compatibility: she dresses up, acts coyly and coquettishly, is gentle and compliant, and ultimately, submits to the male. He, in turn, has to maintain a fairly tough exterior in order to justify his claims to be the exclusive provider and protector.

The reader can no doubt see the historical analogy that follows easily from this scenario. Contemporary hunters battle it out in the economic jungle and their prospective childminders have the benefits of *Miss Selfridge, Chanel No. 5* and *Naughty Nighties* to back up their innate allure. But, according to the sociobiologists, the games we play and the romance we project in the course of our sexual liaisons are surface manifestations of deeper biological determinants:

> Sexual love and emotional satisfaction of family life can be reason-ably postulated to be based on enabling mechanisms in the physi-ology of the brain that have been programmed to some extent through the genetic hardening of this compromise. (Wilson 1978; 139–140)

It will not be possible here to give a full appraisal of this theory and of critical reactions to it. It is fair to say that, despite a certain intuitive appeal due to the superficial congruence of the theory with stereo-typical patterns of heterosexual courtships in Western societies, not a lot of evidence is available to support it. It also has some ideological liabilities which, as the reader may know or guess, have not led to its ready acceptance among feminist thinkers. But still more basic problems with the account as currently formulated are:

(a) that it confounds contemporary social presuppositions with supposedly detached accounts of biology and evolution (Sayers 1982);

(b) that it seems to ignore the fact that evolution has not stopped, and that human beings' clearest evolutionary strength has always been their ability to adapt to changes in the environ-ment (Nicholson 1984);

(c) that it is a reductionist theory which attempts to account for complex phenomena by recourse to lower level principles; and

(d) evidence that social relations may be *organized* around biology
(e.g. around reproduction) is not evidence that they are
determined by biology (Sayers, in press).

Biological accounts and television

Biological theories do not all discount the possible contribution of
social (or para-social) experience to the sex role acquisition process,
but they rarely attribute major influence to such input. Sex roles are,
according to these theories, preprogrammed by nature. Thus, mass
media images are not extensively discussed in the biological literature. However, I think it is possible to identify some predictions that,
if not always made explicit within biological theories, are at least
logically consistent with them and are certainly of some interest to a
general inquiry into the place of TV in sex role transmission.

Essentially, a biological account would predict that the media,
like other human products, will *reflect* underlying (biologically-given)
processes and constraints upon social behaviour. Images in the media
should approximate to the enduring principles of social organization,
time-honoured since the early hunters. Television, the latter day
painting on the cave wall, should exhibit the 'genetic hardening' of the
species. Hence, we would expect TV to provide recurrent images of
strong hunters and their dependent, decorative females. Clearly,
there is much evidence that is consistent with precisely such a
view.

Beyond this, there are a few systematic attempts to deal specifically with the media within a biological framework, though some
occasional claims have been made which verge on the preposterous.
For example, Hutt (1972) pointing to evidence of sex differences in
visual acuity remarks that 'The sensitivity first evident in the cradle is
amply exploited by the strip-teaser and the pornographer' (1972:83).
Quite apart from perpetuating the sex stereotyped myth that arousal
to pornography is a male preserve, it is difficult to see what functional
link there could be between subtle differences on measures of spatial
development in childhood and later sexuality. There do appear to be
some puzzling differences between male and female children's per-
formance in gauging, say, the water level in tilted vessels, but it would
take quite a bit of imagination to relate this to adult male interest in
the line of descent of a stripper's underwear!

Overall, then, the biological theorist is less preoccupied with the
media than are other approaches, but the general position would
seem to be that the media are seen as *reflecting* reality, or 'public
opinion' (cf. Hutt 1978:190), which itself is the surface manifestation
of biological undercurrents. The effects of the media are not usually

discussed, but are presumably expected to be no more than echoes of socialization activities predetermined by nature.

Environmental approaches

In contrast to biological perspectives, which tend to emphasize internal predeterminants, theorists adopting environmental approaches to the explanation of sex roles lay much greater stress on the impact of external factors. While the data concerning biologically-orientated claims, such as the alleged greater activity in male neonates, are often unclear and contradictory (cf. Archer and Lloyd 1982), there is quite reliable evidence that most societies maintain strong (stereotyped) expectations about sex differences from infancy onwards, and it is often argued that these expectations influence dramatically the behaviour and opportunities that children encounter from their earliest days.

In general, environmental theorists propose that these external forces act upon the child to 'shape' or 'mould' her or him into societally-approved ways of behaving. With respect to the development of sex roles, environmentalists frequently point to the accumulating findings that even before a child is born, its parents are likely to have preferences and expectations about its sex (Hoffman 1977), that when it is born it will be perceived as possessing physical, personality and behavioural characteristics in line with societal stereotypes about its gender well before most of these characteristics can be reliably distinguished (Rubin *et al.* 1974) and that from its earliest months onwards it will be immersed in cultural expectations about what it will do and what it will like. There are some well-known and imaginative research demonstrations, for example, that adults behave differently towards an infant according to the gender label that they have been told is appropriate: if adults are given a baby dressed in blue and called 'John' they tend to play more vigorously with 'him', and to hand him more stereotypically masculine toys than do adults presented with the same child in a pink dress and called 'Mary', who is more likely to receive gentler handling, more smiles and more cuddly toys (Seavey *et al.* 1975; Smith and Lloyd 1978).

Variants of environmental theories, drawing on evidence such as the above, can be found in several social science disciplines, including sociology, social anthropology, social and developmental psychology, and they are often manifest in lay thinking about social behaviour. Not all of these accounts specify exactly how these environmental considerations come to influence the child, and quite often the evidence is simply listed on the apparent assumption that the demonstrable pervasiveness of sex stereotyping 'explains' its effects. Rather than discuss environmental theories in general, the essence of the approach having been indicated, it will be more useful to focus briefly on a particular model which has been worked out in greater detail and which has been particularly influential among psychologists interested in media effects, namely Social Learning Theory.

Social Learning Theory is the most systematic and cogent of the environmental theories, and has more interest for psychologists because it attempts to deal with the factors affecting the acquisition and manifestation of social constraints. The overall concern of Social Learning Theory is to explain the relationship between external stimuli and human behaviour (Bandura 1969; Mischel 1966). It postulates that the same learning principles underlie any aspect of an individual's behaviour and that the major principles can be specified as *reinforcement, observation* and *imitation*.

Reinforcement is a concept which reflects the origins of Social Learning Theory in American behaviourism, the dominant school of psychology in North America from the 1920s to the 1950s. Behaviourists have a longstanding interest in the effects of reward (positive reinforcement) and punishment (negative reinforcement) upon an organism's behaviour, and much of this branch of psychology has been concerned with specifying the precise relationship between amounts of reinforcement and the degree of learning that results. Social Learning Theorists apply similar notions to human learning about social behaviour. The implications for the study of sex role learning are obvious: it is pointed out that parents and other socializing agents reward (by praise, affection, toys, etc.) sex-appropriate behaviours such as rough-and-tumble play in boys and doll play in girls from a very early age, and that they punish (by disapproval, discouragement, physical or verbal abuse, etc.) any sex-inappropriate behaviours, especially in boys.

One of the major contributions of Social Learning Theory, however, is its emphasis upon *observation*. Bandura (1969) pointed out that learning processes dependent solely upon reinforcement mechanisms would be a rather uneconomic way of transmitting the full range of human social behaviours. Skinner had shown that one of the most powerful ways of inducing animal learning was to wait for a behaviour to occur spontaneously and then to reinforce it. This is fine when one is working with a laboratory rat in a box, but human parents might have to wait a long time before their child spontaneously engaged in appropriately socially desirable activities which could then be rewarded. Bandura argued that a much faster way to learn was to watch others and observe what kinds of reinforcement they obtain for specific behaviours. Social Learning Theory has been principally concerned with the ways and the conditions in which modelled behaviours influence the observer.

With respect to sex differences, it is clear that the normal child will have considerable opportunity to observe the sex-typed behaviours of adults and older children: at home, at school, and also on television. Mischel (1966) argues that given this opportunity the child learns to *discriminate* between sex-typed behaviour patterns, noticing that some behaviours are performed by males and some by females, and then the child learns to *generalize* from these specific observations to new situations, gradually acquiring information about what is appropriate for each sex and becoming able to label behaviours as 'for boys' or 'for girls'.

One other important feature of Social Learning Theory is the distinction it draws between *observing* and *imitating*. This distinction seems obvious but is easily overlooked in popularized accounts of learning by 'conditioning'. Children generally have the opportunity to observe both sexes and, if they do learn by observing, then both girls and boys have the scope to learn both female and male behaviours. In fact, common sense predicts that they do exactly that. As Mischel (1966:59) points out, the outcome is that 'Men know how to apply face powder, and women know how to place cigars in their mouths', but the probabilities of men and women engaging in these activities are not equal. There is a critical distinction between *acquiring* a behaviour, in the sense of learning how to do it by watching others, and actually *performing* that behaviour oneself. Another major interest for social learning theorists, therefore, has been to discover the conditions under which a given behavioural skill is likely to be performed.

Environmental accounts and television

Because of its emphasis upon the acquisition of information by observation, Social Learning Theory obviously has more potential relevance to the study of media effects than a biological theory might be expected to have. Indeed, much of the experimental work arising from the Social Learning paradigm has been concerned with the effects of film and televised models upon children's behaviour. The classic work on the effects of violence in the media, for example, has been influenced by issues emanating from Social Learning Theory and from Bandura's early experiments (Bandura *et al.* 1963). However, perhaps surprisingly, given the intuitive correspondence between this school of thought and some popular ideas about media effects, not a great deal of work has been done to examine the implications of the theory for our understanding of the contributions of the media to sex role acquisition.

This may be due partly to the waning fortunes of the theory within

psychology: for various reasons, developmental and social psychologists have become increasingly disenchanted with theories which
emphasize external influences and, instead, have become increasingly preoccupied with theories which offer accounts of the internal,
intrapsychic processes of social agents. Social Learning Theorists
themselves have largely capitulated to the 'cognitive revolution'
which swept psychology in the 1960s and 1970s. But a further
reason may be that it is difficult to draw strong predictions from
Social Learning Theory about the effects of the media upon sex
role development. This assertion may seem rather incongruous
with the outline of the theory given above, but it does appear to be
consistent with Mischel's (1966) influential exposition. Mischel
argues:

> The extent to which the child is exposed to same-sex
> models may vary considerably, but in most cultures, and certainly in
> ours, exposure to models of both sexes is sufficient for the child to
> acquire many responses from the repertoires of both sexes.
> (1966:59)

Whether Mischel intended to include the mass media as part of the
exposure for the typical child in Western cultures is a moot point (he
does refer to film and TV models later in the paper (1966:74)) but on
reflection, he is clearly correct in assuming that any child who has
systematic contact with other human beings will have *sufficient* exposure to models of both sexes.

    Thus, it is not clear whether Social Learning Theory would expect
the media to have a strong role to play in the acquisition of sex role
behaviour. Certainly the media present models, and they do so very
effectively, in attention-grabbing formats. But sex is a fundamental
social dichotomy that enters into all human communities in ways
which make it very salient in the everyday life of any child. Notice that
this is rather different from violence, which may be a feature of some
children's everyday lives, but rarely on the scale that the same
children (and all others in less unfortunate circumstances) could find
available in their mass media. Hence, the media may provide a
primary source of information about gangland murders, the Second
World War and the practice of genocide, but much of what they tell
you about everyday male and female behaviour may be more readily
accessible elsewhere.

    Among the problems facing the Social Learning Theory account
of sex role development in general are the findings that measures of
children's sex role orientation do not correlate strongly with those of
their presumed primary models, their parents, and that even the
supposed differential treatment of boys and girls by parents is not as
consistent nor as far-reaching as might be thought (Maccoby and

Jacklin 1974; see Frieze *et al.* 1978: Ch. 6, for a useful discussion). In
the light of these considerations, phenomena extrinsic to the family,
such as TV characters, are sometimes mentioned (e.g. Frieze *et al.*
1978:103–4) as influences whereby children come to reflect broader
cultural standards than those of their own homes. Some content
analysts draw on Social Learning Theory in this way, extrapolating
from studies of violence to the hypothetical effects of sex stereotyping,
claiming that the theory provides 'reason to expect that certain
themes, particularly as they reflect larger cultural values, will be
taught, reinforced and maintained by the television medium' (Levinson 1973:562). In the terms of mass communications researchers (see
Chapter 1), the theory lends itself to incorporation in 'effects' models.
We will see in Chapter 4 that others have drawn similar inferences
from Social Learning Theory.

In short, the Social Learning Theory of sex role development does
claim that models are important sources of information. Television is
one source of models, and some modelled behaviour may be expected
to be rendered especially salient and attractive to the child by virtue of
the technical qualities of the medium. This suggests interesting
considerations for experimental study, but does not really promote a
particularly powerful account of how everyday viewing should contribute to sex role acquisition, relative to other socializing factors.
Interestingly, Mischel himself, in later comments upon sex role
stereotyping in children's media (Mischel 1976:342), simply notes the
iniquity of bias as exposed by content analyses: but advances no
claims about the effects of this bias.

Finally, because Social Learning Theory is a developmental – that
is, it posits that the processes of learning are essentially the same at
any age and for any phenomenon – it does not offer a very strong
account of changes in the salience of models as the child grows
older. This means that investigators who draw loosely upon the
theory in investigating sex role stereotypes, for example when con-
ducting content analyses, tend to overlook the fact that modelled
behaviours, especially by *adults*, in TV may not be understood
identically by children at different stages of development.

Overall, the environmental theories concur that TV is one of
numerous possible external factors impinging upon sex role development. However, it is less easy within these theories to specify just how
important a factor TV might be and its explanatory status seems to
fluctuate even within the most rigorous approach, Social Learning
Theory. The effects of TV on sex role development were not addressed in detail in the influential early discussion of this perspective
by Mischel (1966), though *assumptions* about the medium's
influence tend to have grown since, as evidence for other supposed
causal variables has diminished.

Cognitive-developmental approaches

As we have seen, there are various ways in which we might attempt to explain how an individual arrives at the appropriate sex role. But so far an important question has been overlooked: how does the individual *know* which sex he or she is? To the adult, this seems an extraordinary question, but a moment's reflection makes clear its developmental importance. A child does not 'know' at birth that it is a 'boy' or a 'girl', but has to discover this fact and its implications during early childhood. The 'implications' of being a boy or girl are much less obvious to a toddler even when the child has found out his or her basic category. For example, while it seems obvious to an adult woman that she was once a baby girl, it is far less evident to her two-year-old sister that she will eventually be a woman too. Indeed, the two-year-old has little concrete evidence to be sure that she will become a grown-up of either gender, or even that she will become anything other than a two-year-old.

When we raise these kinds of issues, they bring us to the question of central interest to cognitive-developmental psychologists: how does the child come to know anything at all? Cognitive-developmental theorists are interested in the progress the child makes from a relatively uninformed, prelinguistic infant, through the various levels of childhood sophistication, to the independent reasoning capacities of the adult. Most work in this area is influenced by Piaget's theory of child development, which holds that the child learns by acting upon the environment and organizing the discoveries that result from its actions into increasingly sophisticated mental structures. Piaget spent a lifetime working out his model of the stages of cognitive development and tested it with reference to many aspects of childhood thought, from understanding of the relationships of objects in space and time through the cognitive demands of educational curricula. This is agreed by most psychologists to be one of the major theories of the development of mind, and it dominates child psychology in its effects upon supporters and critics.

Piaget himself did not study the acquisition of sex roles. Indeed, despite the importance of social interaction as a motivating force in his theory, he paid only modest attention to social development. However, one of the most influential theories of sex role acquisition, that of Kohlberg (1966), adapted a basically Piagetian framework to the particular topic of sex roles and this work has provided a seminal reference point for cognitive-developmentalists interested in the topic.

Kohlberg proposed an account of sex role development that 'starts directly with neither biology nor culture, but with cognition' (1966:82). He argued that the child's understanding of sex roles

> is rooted in the child's concept of physical things – the bodies of himself and of others – concepts which he relates in turn to a social order that makes functional use of sex categories in quite culturally universal ways. (1966:82)

According to Kohlberg, the child's first important achievement in this area of social development is the gradual awareness that she or he is a member of a particular sex. Once children have attained this basic social category, they begin to use sex as a basis for categorizing the world, including other people and the kinds of objects, activities and even ideas that are associated with each gender. What is distinctive about the cognitive-developmental account of these processes is the insistence that they are active, in that the child *seeks* information, and that they are systematic or structured, in that the child imposes categories upon the raw data of experience.

The strongest evidence that children are active and structuring in these developments comes from the mistakes that they make and from the gaps in their knowledge. For example, by about age six most children appear to hold very rigid and mutually exclusive sets of beliefs about what the sexes can or cannot do (Kohlberg 1966; Ullian 1976). This development is often particularly galling to parents who espouse non-sexist ideologies and attempt to bring their children up in non-stereotyped ways (and, in my experience, they usually blame this untoward traditionalism in their offspring on the TV).

A number of studies charting the development of children's sex role knowledge have begun to illustrate the gaps and the route of progress in this area of social understanding. Thompson (1975), for example, questioned two- to three-year-olds on their knowledge of their own sex membership and various associations of each sex. While most two-year-olds could indentify their own sex, they were less successful in specifying the sex of other people, and even three-year-olds revealed difficulties in predicting what sex they would be when they grew up, or in identifying sex-typed objects appropriately.

One particularly important test has been developed by Emmerich *et al.* (1977), who were concerned to discover when children attain an understanding of gender constancy, that is the knowledge that a person's gender is an enduring property despite superficial changes in the person's appearance. These kinds of problems are of central interest to cognitive-developmentalists. A better known but related example is the classic Piagetian experiment in which a child watches liquid being transferred from one of two identical beakers containing

identical amounts into a third beaker, which is taller and thinner than
the others. The *amount* of water is unchanged but its *appearance* is
markedly different. Children aged below six or seven years, in what
Piaget calls the preoperational stage, often claim that the amount of
water has been changed, seemingly unable to discount the perceptual
evidence and lacking an awareness of the constancy of the volume:
they fail to 'conserve'. (The explanation of this common finding is
controversial, but the fact that children show developmental differences in their responses to the task is not.)

Emmerich *et al.* developed an analogous test of gender constancy
in which a cartoon figure of a child (named as 'Janie' or 'John') is
presented on a flip pad, and as the experimenter turns the pages, the
child undergoes some change in appearance. Thus, Janie first appears
in long hair and a dress – clearly a female sketch. Her name and sex
are established. Then, the experimenter turns the page to a picture of
the same person with one visible change, say a hair cut. The child is
asked: 'If Janie has her hair cut short like this, what would she be?
Would she be a girl or would she be a boy?' In successive pictures,
'Janie' is presented in boys' clothes or engaging in stereotypically
masculine activities. Similar transformations in the reverse direction
can be made from 'John'. To the adult, it is obvious that a person
retains her or his gender, notwithstanding a change of hairstyle,
clothing or activity. Intriguingly, Emmerich *et al.*'s tests with
thousands of four- to seven-year-olds suggest that this constancy is
much less obvious to young children – even the seven-year-olds were
frequently unsure or incorrect.

The particular interest of Emmerich *et al.*'s work for the cognitive-
developmentalist is, then, that it draws on an analogy between the
development of gender constancy and the development of other
constancies, such as volume, weight and so on, which are known from
work in the Piagetian tradition to be developing during the years four
to eight. Just as the transfer of water in the beakers experiment
involves a perceptual transformation, which seemingly deceives most
preoperational children, so Emmerich *et al.* confronted children with
the perceptual transformation of Janie or John. The results are
consistent with the cognitive-developmentalist's claim of general
cognitive attainments underlying the growth of understanding. Kohlberg and other workers in this paradigm hold that sex roles are
constructed as the child's abilities for discovering and organizing
information develop. The attainment of gender constancy is a key
achievement because it establishes an enduring schema around which
the child can elaborate and extend its knowledge of the subtle
demands imposed upon each sex. Ullian (1976) offers a detailed
account of the stages of development in this respect (see Archer and
Lloyd (1982) and Sayers (in press) for further discussion).

Some problems in the cognitive-developmental framework

Piaget sees continuity between the discovery-based cognitive development of the child and the procedures of a scientist, and so he and many researchers interested in his ideas (whether as followers or critics) have tended to adopt the metaphor of the child as a sort of mini-scientist driven, by an adaptive drive towards mastery of the environment, continuously to test and refine his or her theories of the world. This is an attractive metaphor, capturing the centrality of the child's own mental organization and reorganization to the growth of understanding. However, the metaphor itself tends to neglect account of the extent to which scientific activity is a *social* process, and consequently it has become associated with rather individualistic and hence rather restrictive conceptions of child development.

This leads to at least three substantial problems when we consider cognitive-developmental frameworks in relation to aspects of social development, such as sex roles. First, it minimizes the treatment of the relationship between the child's development and the surrounding culture (cf. Frieze *et al.* 1978:130f.). Cognitive-developmentalists are interested in universal features of development that supposedly underlie the child's treatment of specific phenomena in a specific context. Consequently, the details of a system of knowledge are rather less focal to a cognitive-developmental study than the principles whereby any system of knowledge is constructed. As Bem (1983) points out, cognitive-developmentalists ask important questions about *how* a child comes to categorize the social environment with reference to gender, but tend to ignore the question of *why* they seize upon this particular category in the first place. It is clearly not a coincidence that children come to adopt social conventions related to those of their surrounding community, and it is clearly very important to an account of a given child's social development to explain the congruence between her constructions and the world about her.

Secondly, but closely related to the first point, is the fact that cognitive development almost invariably proceeds in a social (interactive) context, and with respect to social roles this interaction provides simultaneously for the enactment and the discovery of interpersonal regulations. Thus, the metaphor of the individual hypothesis-tester, while relevant to parts of these processes, tends to understate the importance of the intermeshing of collective activity in the construction of social role knowledge.

The third problem associated with the standard cognitive-developmental approach is that it tends to disregard *affective* issues. The main emphases of the theory are on 'cold' cognitions, not unlike those expected of the idealized dispassionate scientist (this is perhaps the most vulnerable feature of the metaphor's premises) and they concern formal arrangements of knowledge structures analogous to models in a textbook. This disregards the obvious fact of social relationships that we attach values and feelings to them. It is probably the least contentious claim that the reader will find in this book to say that to most human beings gender categories *matter*: this is so from quite early in childhood, and obviously a useful theory of this aspect of development needs to acknowledge the fact.

Relating developmental and social psychology

It should be stressed that Piaget himself, as the inspirational force of cognitive-developmental psychology, was not wittingly responsible for these areas of relative neglect, and has at various points acknowledged the importance of social interaction to intellectual development. Nevertheless, in order to begin to understand the relationship between the child and the surrounding culture, we need to draw on perspectives afforded by other areas of psychology, especially social psychology and the relatively recent area of inquiry, social cognition. 'Social cognition' refers both to thinking about social phenomena and to the social contexts in which cognition occurs and develops, and these topics have drawn together developmental psychologists and social psychologists to a focus on common theoretical problems. By drawing upon work in these areas we take better account of the fact that sex role development is by definition a *social* process. Specifically, we can identify frameworks within which we can begin to address the three problems identified above.

First, concerning the relationship between the individual and the culture, we have seen in Chapter 1 that at least some social psychologists regard the characterization of the cultural products of a society, especially the social stereotypes that are maintained within it, as an important component of any theoretical attempt to explain the structures of the society and the social relations it fosters. The study of social stereotypes in a mass medium, as discussed in Chapter 2, is a contribution towards this goal – though as also suggested in Chapter 2, this contribution will be still greater when we have available more schematic and more dynamic models of the interrelationships of roles in the social scripts represented in our cultural products. At least as a starting point, however, a social psychological perspective on social stereotypes acknowledges that these are not merely arbitrary bodies of information that each child may have to learn, but they are manifestations of the underlying social structures to which each child must ultimately, one way or another, accommodate.

Secondly, with respect to the interpersonal context within which the child learns about sex roles, the social psychologist's interest in the 'effective diffusion' of stereotypes (Tajfel 1981; see Chapter 1) raises questions that relate directly to the concerns of the developmentalist. These include questions that will be treated more extensively later, but for the moment it is useful to note that recent developmental work on the emergence of social scripts has been premised on the well-supported assumption that the everyday social activities of the very young enmesh them in complex socio-cognitive structures and routine events well before they can articulate or manipulate abstract categorical knowledge (Nelson 1981:97–98). Nelson proposes that children make their early discoveries about the regularities of social life from the routines of social interaction, wherein they are able to find repetitive structures, consistent sequences of events and predictable outcomes. Thus, if we wish to discover how TV contributes to the diffusion of social knowledge among children we need also to consider how the earliest structures of social intercourse themselves influence the interpretation of medium messages: echoing a point from Chapter 1, how do (young) viewers' scripts and mass media scripts interrelate?

The third problem identified above, the neglected *affective* components of role development, remains the least advanced area of current enquiry, even in the social-cognitive field. However, it is clearly the case that the ways in which social behaviour is organized and regulated are, from early childhood, associated with powerful emotional factors, oriented around the concerns of acceptance, approbation, expectations and love (see Hoffman (1983) and Lepper (1983) for more detailed discussions). It is relevant to acknowledge at the outset that gender classifications and gender-appropriate behaviour are invested with strong affective commitments by others and by self. The acquisition of role knowledge is social, not only in terms of content and context, but also in terms of shared values.

These issues have been considered in greater detail than those arising from each of the two other approaches discussed in this chapter, because they illustrate why an overall perspective is needed which preserves the core emphasis of the cognitive-developmental paradigm on the constructive intellectual activities of the child, yet which also takes account of the social nature of development. As indicated earlier, the bias of this text is towards a developmental social psychological account, drawing upon a synthesis of these two sub-disciplines of psychology. Although developmental social psychology is a very recent hybrid and certainly cannot yet be relied upon to provide all the answers, I hope to be able to sketch in later chapters some of the advantages that accrue from treating mass media effects within this broad framework.

Cognitive development, social interaction and television

The cognitive-developmental approach to sex role acquisition offers an important perspective because of the stress it lays on the child's achievement of categorizing itself and other people by gender, and then striving to discover the correlates of gender membership. Following this perspective, the general course of sex role acquisition may be seen as constrained by the child's developing levels of understanding of the social environment. Many psychologists are attracted to this framework because it emphasizes the self-regulations of the inquisitive child, in contrast to depictions of development as the mere accumulation of bits of information presented randomly by external agents of socialization.

For the cognitive-developmentalist, television is seen as one potential source of information that a child may exploit in trying to construct its understanding of the social world. Information about male and female behaviour is available in TV, often in attractive and stimulating formats, and children may make use of it. However, the extent to which they attend to and assimilate such data will be determined by their current cognitive abilities. Notice that this leads to a shift of emphasis from what TV does to children, to what they do with it. In this sense, cognitive-developmental perspectives overlap with 'uses and gratifications' theories in the mass communications literature which, as we saw in Chapter 1, include information seeking as a key 'need' among viewers.

Whilst following the cognitive-developmental emphasis on the active contributions of the child, it has also been stressed here that much of this activity is conducted in the course of social interaction, and that there are good reasons to suppose that the social knowledge the child attains will reflect the structures of the interpersonal activities in which she or he is immersed from infancy. According to this view, the child is properly regarded as a social *participant* rather than as a pawn of biological forces, a victim of social moulding, or a detached investigator of the environment. Thus, we need to consider medium in the context, not only of cognitive attainments, but also in relation to the child's place and involvement in the social structure.

These are complex considerations, yet we have done little more than begin to identify the issues here, primarily because there are still large gaps in scientists' understanding of how all of these processes operate. This sketch may serve to forewarn the reader that it is unduly optimistic to hope that the study of what happens when children encounter social role information in television will be an easy task. It is time now to turn to some of the investigations that have attempted this venture in the expectation of obtaining simple answers.

FOUR

The more you watch, the worse it gets?

The first three chapters have been spent defining concepts and reviewing theories and, notwithstanding academic cautions about the limits of our present state of knowledge, the reader may well wish to hear the answer to a simple question: what effects does watching sex role stereotyping in television have on young viewers? In fact, it is my experience teaching in the area and of reading popular treatments of the topic that many people perceive that the answer is equally simple. Television is, by and large, full of sexist images; children on average, watch a great deal of television; children almost invariably develop traditional sex role stereotypes, and most people grow up to fulfil traditional sex role expectations. The conclusion is compelling: 'Watching a lot of television leads children and adolescents to believe in traditional sex roles' (Tuchman 1978:37).

The conclusion is so compelling, it appears, that many researchers and writers feel it is unnecessary to test it. I have already pointed out that content analysts frequently assume that having exposed the nature of the beast we know only too well what it does to its victims. The expectation that the greater the degree of exposure to a persuasive source the greater the impact, is one which appeals to common sense, and one which finds support in effects theories in mass communications and (according to some interpreters discussed below) in Social Learning Theory in child study. Above all, it is a prospect of such disturbing practical implications for the everyday lives of entire populations that it merits very careful attention.

But careful attention soon leads to the discovery of problems, and this may well be why rather less energy has been devoted to examining the details of these supposed effects than to alerting us to their possibility. One obvious handicap, for example, is that we do not have optimal conditions available for a good experimental test. It would be convenient to be able to divide a random sample of children into two groups, one of which would receive ten years' worth of TV input, and the other would never see a set and, assuming other environmental factors held reasonably constant, to test the children's sex role development at predetermined points throughout the period. Unfortunately, practical and ethical constraints in the real world obstruct the elegant investigations that we might desire. Where we can still find children unexposed to TV, cross-cultural, economic and ideological differences render it nonsensical to attribute any differences concerning social roles to the effects of one variable such as the presence or absence of TV. Where children within Western cultures are denied access to TV, this is usually because of strong social or religious commitments in their parents, which again make single variable comparisons uninformative.

The compromise, of course, is to contrast children who have been exposed to different amounts of TV, through personal choice or family viewing habits. We then have some basis for testing the 'linear effects' hypothesis (see Chapter 1, and Williams 1981) which maintains that the more TV a child watches, the greater the effect; or the more you watch, the worse it gets. This research strategy is a common one in the mass media field. In fact, even this compromise approach faces severe theoretical and practical problems, which we will consider in detail during this chapter, but it is none the less valuable at the early stages of a research effort to collect evidence on the extent to which the key variables seem to be correlated. Since the study of sex roles and television is in its early stages, most exploratory work can provide useful information.

In this chapter, I will review the available studies which have attempted to assess the strength of the relationship between amount of viewing and aspects of children's sex role development. They can be divided into studies which report an association and studies which have failed to find an association, and I will discuss them in that order.

Studies which report an association between amount of viewing and children's sex role beliefs

If the reader were to consult a number of randomly selected, recent introductory textbooks in the fields of developmental psychology, social psychology and women's studies, and took up discussions of sex role development, it is very likely that she or he would find some allusion to the association between viewing TV and learning of traditional role stereotypes. There is a reasonably high probability that either or both of two studies (Beuf 1974; Frueh and McGhee 1975) will be mentioned in this connection, and there is an almost equally high probability that these will be implied or asserted as evidence of TV effects in this area of social development. The studies are important because they were among the earliest attempts to investigate empirically a relationship that was elsewhere merely the subject of speculation. Because of the importance of their concerns, and the readiness with which they have been interpreted as evidence of 'effects', it is perhaps not surprising that they have risen – through the processes of repeated reference and frequent summaries (and summaries of summaries) that indicate researchers' interest and pedagogical convenience – to the status of received wisdom among many interested in this topic. For these reasons, both of the studies (together in Frueh and McGhee's case with some of their later work) will be considered in some detail in the following sections.

Beuf (1974)

Beuf (1974) interviewed 63 three- to six-year-olds about their television viewing habits and their expectations about adult roles. She classified the children as *heavy viewers* or *moderate viewers*, and reported that 76% of heavy viewers versus 50% of moderate viewers selected sex stereotyped careers for themselves. This finding is regularly summarized in the related literature as evidence of the influence of TV on children's sex role attitudes. Unfortunately, there are some serious drawbacks to the methodology used in the study.

First of all, children in this age range are not wholly reliable as informants on their own viewing times. Self-report, based on unchecked recall, is a weak measure even with adults (if you have regular access to a set, can you remember how many hours TV you saw last week?), and the problems increase the younger the viewer. To work out your weekly viewing time, you have to calculate your daily viewing time seven times and add them up, or once and multiply by seven. Many three-years-olds cannot yet count to seven, let alone add or multiply. Thus, quite how valid Beuf's division of the children into 'heavy' and 'moderate' viewers may be is open to speculation. But if three-year-olds have difficulty in remembering their viewing activity over the last few days, how would we expect them to fare with predictions about their occupational choices some 14 or more years hence? Three- to six-year-olds have quite limited conceptions of future time-spans on this scale. Investigators of the development of vocational interests regard the period up to approximately seven years as a 'fantasy' stage (Super 1957).

It seems very likely that Beuf's subjects were in exactly this stage of career awareness. One child, whom Beuf describes as a 'blond moppet', declared that when she grew up she wanted to 'fly like a bird'. Although the child surmised this was a more likely occupation for boys, the extent to which such aspirations can be legitimately scored as sex stereotyped is questionable.

There are further difficulties with the report in that Beuf does not tell us what cut-off point was used in determining whether the child was categorized as a 'heavy' or 'moderate' viewer, nor how many of the children were placed in each category, nor what the statistical significance of these undisclosed figures is. After all, two groups of individuals divided on *any* arbitrary criterion will display some variation in terms of career preference: we need a statistical analysis to help us decide whether the pattern of choices differs significantly from that which might be expected on the basis of chance and natural fluctuation.

Another problem is that three- to six-year-olds are not an homogeneous group. Children make substantial socio-cognitive developments during these years, and any theory of development will acknowledge that six-year-olds are generally better able to answer questions than three-year-olds. This does not mean, however, that their responses will be invariably more accurate. For example, it is conceivable that one three-year-old interviewee will have only a vague memory of how much TV she has been watching lately, while a five-year-old might remember vividly two cartoons that he enjoyed the previous evening. The salience of these brief exposures may outweigh his actual viewing time when asked at school the next day how much TV he watches.

Five- to six-year-olds may thus report higher viewing times because they actually *have* higher viewing times, or because they have stronger recall of enjoying their viewing, or both. If this reasoning is correct, the 'heavy' viewers in Beuf's sample may have included disproportionate numbers of the older children. Now, older children in this age range, for independent reasons, may be better able to answer questions about adult occupations, and may be more sex-typed as a function of general or specific developmental processes (see Chapter 3). Again, if this reasoning is correct, the 'heavy' viewers may have been older, more able to answer questions from a strange adult and, perhaps, more sex-typed. Beuf does not consider these possible confounding factors, and her data do not allow us to attempt to disentangle them.

Nevertheless, Beuf infers that

The television viewing data indicate that the *more* children see of the world, as it is presented by everyday cultural purveyors, the more likely they are to apply sex stereotypes to careers (1974:144).

She suggests that the stereotyped media to which children are exposed may be the reason why these children of the 1970s, born 'since the beginning of the women's movement' (1974:142), are resistant to liberated conceptions of sex roles. Yet in describing the domestic backgrounds of these subjects she reports that they are typically from nuclear families with fathers in traditionally male occupations and mothers who are non-wage earning housewives. Perhaps it is not only the TV in these households which is resistant to liberation!

I think we have to conclude that Beuf's study does not provide strong evidence of an association between TV viewing and sex role stereotyping in children. Such an association may exist but this particular investigation does not expose it. The study made a contribution as an early attempt to seek out such a link and to raise questions for further research but it is not in itself persuasive.

The McGhee and Frueh studies

Another investigation that is commonly mentioned alongside Beuf's work is that of Frueh and McGhee (1975). This is a one-page report of an interesting project attempting to test the relationship between amount of viewing and a measure of traditional sex role orientation. The length of the report is relevant because it is worth stressing that, as concise and well-ordered an article as Frueh and McGhee's is, it cannot discuss all of the possible implications and interpretations of their work in such a short space; hence, subsequent citations have been based on the briefest of summaries and, as we will see, the evidence is not as overwhelming as is sometimes supposed.

Frueh and McGhee designed their study well. Their subjects were 40 boys and 40 girls, with 10 of each sex sampled at each of four age levels (approximately, four to six years, eight years, 10 years and 12 years). Measures of viewing time were compiled by parents for the two younger age groups and by the children themselves (with some parental checking) in the older groups. The children were also administered the 'It Scale' (Brown 1956), a projective test in which the child is provided with a drawing of a stick figure (It), and asked to select, from a series of pictures of objects with sex stereotyped associations, those objects which the It would prefer. The test is based on the assumption that the child's choices for It reflect the child's own preferences 'projected' into the figure. To the extent to which these preferences are consistent, the test is supposed to provide a measure of the strength of the respondent's sex role preference.

The significant findings were as follows: high TV watchers obtained higher It Scale scores; boys obtained higher scores than girls; higher scores were obtained with increasing age. The authors conclude:

> high amounts of television watching are clearly associated with stronger traditional sex role development . . . this relationship holds equally for boys and girls, and it does not change with increasing age. (Frueh and McGhee 1975)

Unfortunately, Frueh and McGhee do not present a full table of means (and give no indication of the range around the means), so that it is difficult to know what to make of the fact that It scores, age, and viewing hours were apparently intercorrelated. They analyse their results by analysis of variance (a statistical test of the significance of differences among means) while it would be equally or more useful to have some indication of the strength of the association between amount of viewing and It scores when the association between amount of viewing and age had been taken into account. We know that children develop increasingly traditional sex role beliefs during these years, and we know that their television viewing increases: Frueh and McGhee (1975) do not clarify the causal relationships among these developments.

However, there are other, more fundamental problems with the study, particularly with the instrument used to measure strength of sex role development, the It Scale. There are technical weaknesses with this measure which undermine its validity (Eisenberg 1983), particularly with children aged over seven or so. For example, Paludi (1981) has found that the method has a male bias, and so Frueh and McGhee's finding of higher scores among boys could possibly be a reflection of this. Eisenberg (1983), in a detailed critique of this instrument, points out that a basic problem with the It test is that it is unclear whether it is a measure of the respondent's *own* sex role orientation or the respondent's knowledge of sex role regularities *in general*. Above all, the reader does not need to be a specialist in test design and psychometrics to see that it is quite a leap from a guessing game about the toy activities and preferences of a matchstick person to the assumption that this reflects the general sex role outlook of the child. Taking Frueh and McGhee's results at face value, and disregarding the possible influence of any other variable in the child's life, it could be that their results indicate some association between high TV viewing and the desire to introduce consistency into the recreational preferences of stick figures. This may be interesting to specialists but it is not in itself an indictment of TV exposure.

Frueh and McGhee's report is an important one in this field
because it did pioneer attempts to quantify the relationship between
amount of viewing and degree of sex typing. In the state of knowledge
on this topic in the early 1970s, not many relevant measures existed
and few previous findings were available as guidelines. Nevertheless,
the findings are not clear cut and on even the most generous interpretation can do no more than hint at an association. It is interesting
to reflect that this has not prevented frequent citation of the study as
evidence of effects, a view endorsed by McGhee and Frueh (1980)
themselves in aligning their evidence with Social Learning Theory:

> While this study [Frueh and McGhee 1975] is subject to the normal
> constraints on interpretation of correlational data, the demon-
> strated significance of observational learning [Bandura 1969;
> Mischel 1970] combined with the high amount of children's ex-
> posure to this learning source, suggest that television is likely to
> have *contributed importantly* to children's learning of sex role
> stereotypes. (McGhee and Frueh 1980:181; my emphasis)

The normal constraints on the interpretation of correlational data
are of course that (a) the fact that two variables are correlated could
be due to the presence or influence of a third variable, and (b)
correlation does not demonstrate causation which, if it is involved,
could operate in either direction (for example, highly stereotyped
children could opt to watch more television because it matches their
distorted view of the world better than reality does). By alluding to
'normal constraints' McGhee and Frueh seem to feel they have dealt
with them, but their claim still amounts only to a *circumstantial* one,
specifically that children watch a lot of television and children acquire
sex role stereotypes. McGhee and Frueh (1980) continue, inciden-
tally, by citing Beuf's (1974) findings as similar to, and supportive of
their own.

McGhee (1975) does discuss several of the problems associated
with the It Scale in a paper providing a lengthier discussion of the
original work and a summary of an extension of the study conducted
some 15 months later. Although the main pattern of findings in the
extension was apparently similar (McGhee does not provide details of
means), one surprising result was obtained: *low* TV watchers showed
a significantly greater increase in the amount of sex-typing in their
preferences than did high TV watchers. High TV watchers were still
more sex-typed, but light viewers seemed to be increasing their sex
typing (or at least their It scores) at a greater rate.

McGhee explains this incongruous finding as probably due to the
limitations of the It Scale on which, he suggests, the heavy viewers
had reached a 'ceiling effect' by the first data collection point. The top
score on the test is 84, and the heavy viewing children had a mean
score of 71·5. It is not obvious why a standardized test should have a

range of over 12 points above the ceiling, but if 71·5 is the average top
score then one wonders if, in the original analysis, most of the high
scores were found in the oldest, high viewing boys' cell (possibly
undermining the sensitivity of the statistical test used).

However, this quibble becomes redundant in the light of
McGhee's (1975:213) own conclusion that the It Scale is not really
adequate for an investigation with children as old as those used in the
Frueh and McGhee study. This is probably true and of course a
researcher's judgement based upon direct experience is very relevant
to the evaluation of a test instrument. The consequence of McGhee's
observation though, must be to throw further doubt on the claims
made about the study. Hence, we find that this widely cited, if
minimally detailed report, is based around a problematic instrument
and that its less well known follow-up produces some incongruous
findings, indicating greater increases (on the dubious measure)
among *light*-viewing subjects – and that at this point the authors
concluded that the measure was inadequate. We turn now to a later
report.

McGhee and Frueh (1980)

McGhee and Frueh (1980) is a fuller report of the follow-up work,
concentrating on a different test which was also administered, The
Sex Stereotype Measure, developed by Williams *et al.* (1975). This
measure is concerned with children's understanding of the personality characteristics stereotypically associated with the sexes. The child
is shown silhouette figures of a male and a female and asked a series of
questions designed to test which sex is seen as *aggressive, tough, daring,
logical* and so on (i.e. stereotypically male properties) and which is
seen as *gentle, emotional, nagging, soft-hearted* and so on (i.e. stereotypically female attributes). This test obviously focuses on more
profound dimensions of sex role stereotypes than toy preferences.
Given the findings on sex stereotyping in television, familiar from
Chapter 2, which do indicate that on TV males are often cast as
aggressive, tough, and daring and females as gentle, and so on, it is
certainly of interest to discover the relationship, if any, between
amount of viewing and stereotyping as measured by such a test.

Briefly, McGhee and Frueh found that heavy TV viewers made
more frequent stereotyped choices on both male and female items.
Unfortunately, they omit the means and standard deviations for these
results, so that it is not possible for the reader to gauge directly how
substantial these differences are. In this study, the authors found that
female children were overall significantly more stereotyped than
male children though, again, the descriptive statistics are not made

available. Note that this contrasts with the findings of the Frueh and
McGhee (1975) study, where *boys* were found to be more sex typed (on
the It Scale), and remember that these are the same children.

The authors do present means relating to a significant interaction
effect on the male items. The meaning of an interaction effect is that
the influence of one factor varies at different levels of another factor.
In this case, heavy TV viewers showed a progressive increase in
stereotyped responses which level off around age 12, while light
viewers show a progressive decrease through the age range studied.
McGhee and Frueh take this as supporting their general hypothesis
that 'heavy television viewing may contribute significantly to children's acquisition of stereotypic perceptions' (1980:185). It is consistent with the hypothesis, but then the lack of similar findings with
female stereotypes is not. McGhee and Frueh pay much less attention
to the latter. Further, when we look at the mean scores on the Sex
Stereotype Measure, we find that the heavy and light viewing subjects
are never more than three points apart (on a 12-point scale) at any age
level, and usually the difference is less. Among boys, for example,
heavy viewers' highest score is at around age 12, when their mean is
approximately 10·4; light viewing boys at the same age score around
8·6.

Another interesting comparison between the results of the two
main studies is that while Frueh and McGhee (1975) found that light
viewers' scores on the It Scale *increased* with age, McGhee and Frueh
(1980) found that light viewers' Sex Stereotype scores *decreased* with
age. Let me emphasize again that these are the same viewers.
Obviously, two tests providing such discrepant results cannot be
valid measures of the same phenomenon. For reasons indicated
above, I think the authors were justified in abandoning the It Scale. It
is curious that by 1980 McGhee and Frueh had grown more confident
that their 1975 study indicated an important contribution of TV to
sex role stereotyping in children, even though they had by 1980
discarded the measure used in 1975. Indeed, McGhee and Frueh
(1980) made no mention at all of the *second* administration of the It
Scale, and one has to read the less well known paper by McGhee
(1975) for a discussion of this.

This leaves us with the partial support that McGhee and Frueh
derive from the scores on the male items in the 1980 report. To
recapitulate, these are contradicted by the absence of similar findings
on the female items, and they do not amount to large differences in
any case.

McGhee and Frueh (1980) actually offer an explanation for the
differences between heavy and light viewers on the male scores which
contradicts their original hypothesis of observational learning from TV.
They suggest that both types of viewers have similar levels of stereo-

typic perceptions of males at age seven, and that heavy viewing 'may simply strengthen perceptions of males which have *already been formed apart from mass media influences*' (1980:186; my emphasis). The light viewer on the other hand 'may be more able to learn from his (her) own experience, and decide that so-called masculine traits or characteristics may actually be associated with either sex' (1980:187). In other words, the 'important' and 'significant' contribution that McGhee and Frueh had detected on pp. 181 and 185 of their article (see quotations above) had become minimal by pp. 186–7.

To summarize: the (1975) study and the (1980) study produce mutually incongruous results; part of the resolution of these is to admit that the earlier study was based on a weak measure; this means we cannot take the 1975 study as demonstrating a meaningful association; the (1980) study uses a better measure but produces inconclusive results, which lead the investigators themselves to a revised position, now minimizing observational learning from television as an explanation of sex role stereotyping in children.

I have one prediction to volunteer here, and it is that Beuf (1974), Frueh and McGhee (1975) and McGhee and Frueh (1980) will continue to be cited frequently as evidence of the 'effects' of sexist television content. My own conclusion is that this amounts to a misrepresentation of their findings. It is interesting to consider why the research community has been so amenable to superficial accounts and interpretations of these works, and I return to this point at the end of this chapter. First, however, it will be useful to draw the reader's attention to several other correlational studies that seem to have attracted rather less enthusiasm.

Some studies which have failed to find an association between amount of viewing and sex role stereotyping in children

Perloff (1977) classified 160 young adolescents as light (0–24·5 hours per week), moderate (25–34·5 hours) and heavy (35–54 hours) viewers on the basis of questionnaire responses. He gave the children and their parents a Sex Role Stereotype questionnaire and examined the relationship between the amount of viewing and scores on the latter. No effect of television was found.

Perloff comments on the discrepancy between his findings and Frueh and McGhee's (1975) results, and suggests that it may be that the Sex Role Stereotype measure was too abstract and that the It Scale may be more appropriate. We need not review the problems of the It Scale again, but will simply recall that McGhee (1975) himself had already argued in the opposite direction, that the It Scale was too insensitive with children over age seven or so, and note that Perloff's young adolescent subjects should possess the conceptual and linguistic abilities necessary to understand the meaning of personality characteristics focused upon in a Sex Role Stereotype questionnaire. Perloff *did* find an association with maternal employment: children whose mothers were employed outside the home had less stereotyped views.

Meyer (1980) tested 150 girls aged six to eight and 10 to 12 years. Amount of television viewing was determined from independent estimates by mother and daughter of the number of hours the child watched TV during an average week. Four measures of the child's sex-role attitudes were taken: an activities list (activities were rated as potentially 'male', 'female', 'both'), a female competence measure, a work desire measure, and a typical day measure. No significant correlations were found between scores on these measures and viewing level. Several of the daughters' sex-role attitudes in Meyer's study *were* significantly associated with maternal attitudes and goals (though not with maternal employment).

Cheles-Miller (1975) gave 276 ten- to 12-year-old children a Stereotype Acceptance Test (SAT) designed to measure acceptance of traditionally stereotyped marital roles in television commercials. Contrary to hypothesis, children scoring high on the SAT watched *less* television (based on self-report measures), and knew less about current television advertising than lower scorers. An interesting, unexpected finding was that low SAT scorers watched a 'good deal of television and (had) a substantial knowledge of television commercials' (Cheles-Miller 1975:47). In short, this study provides indirect evidence to suggest that at least some high television watching children are *more* critical of medium content, especially the stereotypes they observe. More important correlates of SAT scores were the subject's *liking* of television commercials (positively related), the mother's occupational rating (negatively related), and the child's self-concept (negatively related).

Two overall points can be made about the various findings of Perloff's, Meyer's and Cheles-Miller's studies. First, each investigation used considerably larger numbers of subjects than Frueh and McGhee (1975) or Beuf (1974). Since so many factors and so much individual variation can be expected to play parts in as complex a phenomenon as sex role development, it is advisable to use reasonably large samples in correlational designs to avoid picking up spurious relationships or missing authentic associations due to a few extreme respondents. Secondly, although each of these large studies did not find the expected correlation, each showed effects related to domestic factors, such as maternal employment or maternal attitudes.

So far then, we have seen that there are several serious objections to the interpretations that have often been made about two of the better known studies in this field, and we find that there are at least three published investigations, employing larger samples, providing contradictory evidence.

It is interesting, though scarcely surprising, to find that when an investigator takes more variables into account, the results become more complex. Another well-designed correlational study by Zuckerman *et al.* (1980), for example, looked at the relationships among sex role prejudice and several variables including demographic, familial and viewing factors. Again, the sample was a reasonably large one of 155 children with a mean age of 9·4 years. The strongest relevant findings for our purposes were that, where prejudice existed, *among girls* it was moderately associated with the child's lower IQ, the mother's educational level and amount of viewing. These three variables together accounted for 19% of the variance in girls' sex role attitudes. Thus, we see a family background factor (maternal education) involved again, but in any case the findings indicate that 81% of the variance is due to something else. The direct relationship between the amount of TV viewing and sex role prejudice was minimal. Zuckerman *et al.* tested for comparable relationships for boys, and found none.

Repetti (1984) examined possible correlates of five- to seven-year-olds' sex stereotypes concerning toys and occupations. Measures were taken of 40 children's total TV viewing time, as well as the amount of time that the children spent viewing *educational* TV programmes, and their parents' sex role orientations as reflected in BSRI scores (see Chapter 1). No relationship was found between *total* viewing time and sex stereotyping in the children, but amount of viewing of educational TV was *negatively* correlated with stereotyping. That is, the more educational TV a child watched, the lower his or her sex role stereotype score, at least with respect to toys and occupations. This could reflect a deliberate avoidance of sex stereotypes in educational TV (which seems plausible, but see Dohrmann, 1975, discussed in Chapter 2), or possible occasional interventions in this area of the medium deliberately intended to counteract traditional stereotypes (see Chapter 6), or could reflect the possibility that parents who encourage more educational TV viewing also foster less sex-typed practices in other activities at home. Positive associations *were* found in Repetti's study between parental sex role orientations and the children's stereotypes.

The last correlational study I shall discuss in this chapter is one of the largest, with the additional merit that the data were conducted longitudinally, over a two-year period. This is the work of Morgan (1982), a study which set out to examine the relationship between amount of TV viewing and a sample of 349 adolescents' sex role stereotypes. Morgan collected 'sexism' measures (discussed below) from his subjects and found a 'small but significant' (Morgan 1982:953) relationship for girls between the amount of viewing in the second year of the study and their sexism scores one year later. For boys, no such relationship emerged. Morgan then broke down his sample by I.Q., so that correlations between amount of viewing and intensity of sexism could be tested for each sex within each of three I.Q. groups (low, medium and high) at each two data collection points. No clear pattern of results emerged: there were modest significant correlations for medium I.Q. boys in the third year of the study, and weak correlations for high I.Q. girls during both years of the study, but no other associations were found for the boys and girls in the other I.Q. groups at any points.

When positive correlations were obtained, then, they were not strong (ranging from 0·18 to 0·43) and not easy to interpret. Morgan himself discusses them in terms of the 'mainstreaming' hypothesis of Gerbner *et al.* (1980) rather than the linear effects hypothesis, and the reader is referred to his paper for a more detailed account (see also Durkin, 1985b). Rather than debate here the interpretation of the occasional weak to modest relationships reported, however, it is relevant to note that there are some weaknesses in Morgan's study which make these findings still more ambiguous.

First, Morgan provides a review of the previous literature on the effects of cumulative exposure to TV, and remarks that the findings of the studies are 'quite consistent' (1982:948). The studies include an unpublished paper by Kimball (1977) (which, according to Morgan's summary, actually produced internally inconsistent findings), and those of Beuf (1974) and Frueh and McGhee (1975). This is not in itself a weakness in Morgan's design, of course, but it does indicate that the study was based upon some rather insecure assumptions.

Secondly, and this is a design problem, Morgan's measure of sexism was very limited. He used a five-item scale, which is an extremely succinct basis at best for tapping adolescents' sex role attitudes, and one which Morgan himself reports has 'only moderate internal homogeneity' (1982:950): in other words, it is not certain that the test measured reliably exactly what it was supposed to measure. When we look at the scale, some of the reasons for this uncertainty emerge. The subjects were asked the following questions, and the possible answer choices were provided as indicated. The italicized items are deemed, by Morgan, to be 'sexist' answers.

> In a family, who do you think should have full-time jobs – *the father*, the mother, or both?
>
> *True* or false – men are born with more drive to be ambitious and successful than women.
>
> True or *false* – our society discriminates against women.

> *True* or false – by nature, women are happiest when they are making
> a home and caring for children.
>
> *True* or false – women have just as much chance to get big and
> important jobs, but they just aren't interested.
>
> (Morgan 1982:949)

However, it may be misleading to use the term 'sexism' (which
denotes *prejudice* against one or the other sex; see (Chapter 1) to
describe adolescents' agreement with some of these statements. For
example, it is not obvious that perceiving someone as being happy
when caring for children is a negative judgment, though it may
indicate a *stereotyped* belief. To be sure that sexist attitudes were being
measured here we would need an indication that the respondents'
views were prescriptive. For example, their agreement that women
should be happiest when caring for children and that this *should* be at
the exclusion of other personal expression, career attainment, *etc.*
would be a better indicator of prejudice. We would also need to be
sure that respondents did not hold these views of adults in general –
and the adolescents' opinions on men's interests in child care were not
tested. This particular question from the scale has been considered in
detail here because Morgan found (1982:950) that it was the most
consistent source of data among the responses but note that similar
questions could be raised of the less consistent items.

To some extent, these semantic and methodological quibbles may
seem beside the point. Intuitively, it is easy to see the basis for
Morgan's questions and to agree that individual differences in responses to them might reflect something about the subjects' views on
sex roles. However, whether we regard children's responses as sexist
(*i.e.* negatively prejudiced) rather than sex stereotyped (*i.e.* based on
an inaccurate generalization) may have implications for how we
design interventions. Still more importantly for the present discussion, even if we accept that the scale is measuring sex stereotypic
beliefs we have to acknowledge that its relationship with amount of
TV viewing turned out not to be consistent or strong.

Thus, although Morgan's study is one of the most ambitious to
have been reported in this area, like any empirical investigation it
does have drawbacks. And like all of the empirical investigations of
the relationship between viewing time and 'sexism', it does not
provide conclusive results.

Linear effects: the evidence

To summarize, the linear effects hypothesis predicts that the greater
the viewer's exposure to a particular type of message in television, the
stronger the effects. A sensible strategy for testing this hypothesis as it

relates to the present topic is to examine statistically the relationship between the amount of viewing a child engages in and some measure of the child's sex role beliefs or attitudes. Several such tests have been conducted, using a range of measures. None of them has demonstrated a strong or convincing relationship between the two variables. These early findings serve as a warning that the hypothesis is not so self-evidently supportable as is often supposed. It is easy to see why linear effects assumptions have been popular in many discussions of television and sex role acquisition, but we have to face the possibility that there are some weaknesses inherent in this perspective. Several of these will now be outlined.

1. The 'normal constraints on interpretation of correlational data'

As indicated earlier, while correlational findings are interesting they do not demonstrate causality. Even if some future researcher does find a reliable, positive and substantial correlation between exposure and attitude, it can always be interpreted to support different accounts. These include the possibilities that a third variable (or set of variables) is implicated (e.g. parents, viewing choice, social class), and that the causality might be operating in the other direction (strongly stereotyped children might seek out sex-typed TV content).

Thus, if strong correlations were found they would provide *necessary* evidence in support of the linear effects hypothesis, but would not be *sufficient* to support it exclusively.

2. Production and reception are not identical processes

We cannot assume in any form of human communication that encoding by producer and decoding by receiver are mirror–image processes. If they were, there would never be misunderstandings or breakdowns in communication. In the present case, it is a precarious assumption that young children will extract from TV content perfect understanding of the streams of behaviour they observe therein, or even that subliminal fragments of the repetitive stereotypes are somehow 'burned' into their unconscious, accumulating seditiously until they shape irrevocably the viewers' minds into replicas of media images.

3. Frequency is not equivalent to saliency

We can count the number of times per hour that some examples of sex stereotyped representation appears on our screens but this is not a count of how much or how often the representation has an impact upon 'the viewer'. Content analyses exposing sex stereotyping in TV provide 'census-type information' (Greenberg 1982:188), but do not necessarily capture the varying meaningfulness of the information to the audience. Even the very same incident will be appraised differently according to context. Consequently, it is naive to expect that TV input can be characterized as a lump sum invested in the safe of the viewer's mind and stored without further accounts being made.

4. More viewing provides more scope for diversity

As Howitt (1982:98) has pointed out, although more viewing time means more exposure to whatever undesirable properties TV may have, it does also allow for more opportunity to encounter exceptional or non-stereotyped phenomena among its range of programmes. TV is a pluralistic medium, its contents do include conflicting representations of the social world and by virtue of its commitments to be reasonably topical it does accommodate occasionally to new developments and new ideas in the world around it. Thus, although TV remains on balance sex stereotyped, there are *some* non-stereotyped programmes and there is *some* non-hostile coverage of issues pertaining to women's rights, changing roles and so on in both adults' and children's TV – and the more you watch, the more likely you are to encounter it. Given the preceding point about saliency, it is conceivable in principle that these exceptions to the norm are more noticeable and have more impact upon at least some viewers. We return to the issues raised by this possibility in Chapter 6.

5. Overlooking the effects of other variables

No theory or researcher attributes total responsibility to TV for the patterns of sex role development. However, the linear effects hypothesis tends to neglect variations in the possible involvement of other factors (such as parental expectations, siblings, peers, schooling and so on) and takes these implicitly as constants in children's environments. Thus, the only variable assumed to increase or decrease is the amount of TV input the child receives, whereas in practice many aspects of children's environments vary from home to home. As we have seen, there is evidence that some of these (e.g. maternal employment) are associated with variations in sex role attitudes. At the very least the linear effects hypothesis overlooks a perennial problem in media research: by sacrificing more time to TV, what do high-viewing children do less of than their lower watching peers?

6. It is naive to expect the same effects in
different children

Probably the most serious weakness of the linear effects approach to
TV and sex-typing is the atheoretical assumptions it rests upon about
children. At worst, the work assumes that children are empty slates
upon which society writes its message; we have already seen in
Chapter 3 that few developmental psychologists follow this view
because of the wealth of contrary evidence – we will be returning to
some of the broader theoretical issues later (see Chapters 5 and 7), but
for the moment it is worth stressing that much correlational research
has looked for identical 'effects' in children of quite wide age ranges.
This creates methodological problems (such as choosing measures
which give comparable information about five-year-olds and 14-year-
olds), but still more importantly, it obscures or avoids major theoretical issues. Children's *understanding* of TV changes radically through
development, and their *use* of it (relative to other social activities)
changes qualitatively and quantitatively over time. Some correlational designs fail to address these basic developmental considerations, and most make the conceptual leap from a claim about the
particular age group used in a given study to *all* developing people,
from toddlers to adolescents.

Why are linear effects popular?

Finally, it is worth asking briefly why the linear effects model has been
adopted so uncritically in some discussions of TV and sex role
development. This is really an issue for specialists in the sociology of
science but a few observations may be made. First, as already
indicated, the model has a seductive simplicity, and proposes a direct
stimulus–response relationship that has attracted many previous
researchers of media effects in other contexts, and almost invariably
has been found lacking when the evidence was collected. In this
respect, sex role researchers have merely recapitulated elements of the
natural history of media effect research (cf. McQuail 1983:179f.).
This is not in itself undesirable because the information is useful: if it
had been found that viewing time was strongly associated with sex
role attitudes in children then that would certainly have provided
important grounds for policy discussion; equally, the lack of clear
evidence for such an hypothesis informs future research.

Secondly, the linear effects model ties in with those political
ideologies which represent people as the unwitting products of their
environment, and such ideologies are sometimes taken for liberal or

even radical challenges to the *status quo* and therefore have superficial attractions to some critics of inequities in the social system. The obvious liability of these positions is that by metaphorically robbing human beings of a place in the determination of their environments, they demean the species and attribute people the status of malleable plastic. Developing well-meaning but inadequate accounts of the bases of social problems may be a poor, even counterproductive, starting point for attempts to promote change.

Thirdly, and I have to admit that this is no more than a guess, it is conceivable that there is a kind of meta-stereotyping occurring in the social sciences themselves, whereby research into sex roles and related phenomena tends to be perceived (stigmatized) as women's work, and therefore downgraded so that it receives less critical attention. Perhaps this is because it may appear illiberal to question any claims pertaining to research in sexual inequality, and it is probably true to say that anything that smacks of feminism, which sex role research often connotes, tends to be either avoided or patronized by the scientific establishment. This is not to suggest that the research itself is of low quality but rather that certain theoretical presuppositions, such as the notion of unmediated effects, survive for longer in derived accounts of this area than in comparable areas of psychology.

We find, then, that first attempts to answer the simple question with which we started this chapter do not provide the simple answer that might have been convenient. It turns out to be very difficult to measure satisfactorily the relationship between amount of viewing and as complex an aspect of personal development as sex roles. Although it remains possible in principle that some future investigation may address more successfully the methodological and conceptual problems illuminated by recent work, there is scant evidence at present from which to predict that such an idealized investigation would uncover a linear relationship. The best working hypothesis, on the basis of the findings of the several investigations reviewed in this chapter, is that the relationship is not that straightforward.

This is not to refute the possibility that there may *be* a relationship between television viewing and sex role learning, but the evidence and the issues discussed so far lead to the conclusion that it must be a rather complicated one. We turn in Chapter 5 to different approaches to the topic that may help uncover some features of the relationship and point to some of the questions still unresolved.

FIVE

The more you watch, the more you see?

In the previous chapter, we considered a number of studies which attempt to ascertain the relationship between the amount of TV viewing that a child engages in and the degree of sex typing that she or he displays. Although such work is a necessary and important component of the general study of children and television, correlational methodologies have a number of drawbacks which we have now considered at some length. One further drawback of correlational methods based on viewing time measures is that they rarely take account of what happens during *viewing activity*. Indeed, the phrase 'viewing activity' reflects a phenomenon that correlational studies tend to disregard, and one which also may sound self-contradictory to the lay person accustomed to the notion of television viewing as a passive rather than active business. Yet we know from decades of research into the psychology of perception that our monitoring of the environment is very much an active and constructive process (see, e.g. Neisser 1967, 1980) and in recent years researchers have begun to show that this is true of television viewing and, of particular relevance to our concerns in this book, that it is true of *children's* television viewing.

In this chapter, we will examine the fruits of a variety of studies, exploiting different methodologies, which do attempt to investigate what happens when children view sex stereotyped television material. We will consider how children attend to this aspect of television, how they comprehend it, and how they react to it. The overall purpose of the chapter is to indicate that what children bring with them to their viewing will influence substantially what they extract from it.

Attending to television

In most Western societies, contemporary children have some experience of television almost as soon as they appear in the world. The TV is 'on' in most living rooms for several hours per day, and new babies are as likely as other members of the family to spend some time near a set. While it is unlikely that neonates are troubling themselves with decisions such as which TV-advertised shampoo is best suited to their gender profile, it is known that quite early in life infants modify their vocal and visual behaviour according to whether the TV is on or off, whether or not patterned pictures are visible, and whether or not the sound is on (see Hollenbeck and Slaby 1979). During the first two or three years of life, children make quite impressive leaps from these early responses to the box to fairly discriminating viewing patterns. Some of the most interesting recent work on early TV viewing has been conducted by Anderson and his colleagues (Anderson and Levin 1976; Anderson *et al*. 1981; Anderson and Lorch 1983), who point out that at around age two and a half years children reveal an increasingly protracted and structured interest in television.

Anderson *et al*. (1981) argue that young children's attention to television, like their attention to anything else, reflects in part their goals of furthering their developing understanding of their environment. Evidence in support of this perspective includes the fact that children reduce or terminate attention to TV content which is unintelligible to them or is so familiar that they do not need to predict what will happen next. When preschool children are observed in the presence of a TV set with additional activities simultaneously available, they do not devote their attention singly to the box but they vary their visual activity according to the presence or absence of features that interest them. Anderson *et al*. have studied which features elicit and which inhibit attention to TV in such circumstances.

Among other findings, these investigations have revealed that the presence of a woman's voice can serve to draw children's visual attention to the screen, while a man's voice tends to terminate interest. It may be that preschool children, accustomed to female-organized domestic and nursery environments, are alert to the possibility that womens' voices may signal events or announcements of particular interest to them or, a complementary possibility, it may be that children of this age have discovered that the presenters of their favoured programmes are often women. While questions arise here which call for further investigation, the indications that even young viewers' attention to TV is non-random and non-reactive are important. Specifically, they suggest that we should regard the child not as a rote learner but as a purposeful, if still relatively uninformed, student to whom television provides one variable source of data and information.

Attending to social information in television

To some extent, the data and information of television are *intrinsic*: that is, things happen on the screen which viewers find inherently 'watchable' for a variety of reasons. The medium is a multiplicity of messages. But for present purposes the kind of information of greatest relevance is that which bears upon the real world outside of the box, particularly the social world populated by male and female people. What we wish to discover is whether social data *in* the medium are used by young viewers as part of their broader attempts to become informed social beings in the world *outside* of the medium. Do children attend to sex role information in television, and do they incorporate any of it into their social cognitions about this domain of personal attributes?

Although two- to three-year-olds may be more responsive to female voices in certain viewing conditions, most observers of sex role development recognize that slightly later, say around age four to six, children are more aware of their own gender and are more interested in discovering the specific opportunities and constraints that this category membership affords. We have already seen for example (Chapter 3) that during this period children gradually develop what has been termed 'gender constancy', the realization that gender is an enduring personal property with predictable consequences for one's appearance and behaviour. What consequences does this cognitive attainment have for children's attention to male and female figures in TV?

In an important study, Slaby and Frey (1975) set out to examine this relationship between social cognition and viewing preferences. They divided preschool children aged two to five years, according to their scores on a gender constancy test, as at *low* or *high* stages of gender understanding. Each child was subsequently shown a silent colour film depicting an adult male and an adult female simultaneously carrying out a series of simple activities such as building a fire, making popcorn, playing a musical instrument, etc. The models were presented on a split-screen and the child's visual attention to each half of the picture was timed by an observer via a one-way mirror.

Slaby and Frey predicted that children at the *high* levels of gender constancy would devote more attention to the same-sex model. This was exactly what was found among the boys, and the pattern for the girls was in the expected direction, though not statistically significant.

Attention to same-sex actors does appear, in this study, to be at least partially determined by the child's level of gender constancy. Following Kohlberg's (1966) account of sex role development (see Chapter 3), Slaby and Frey (1975) suggest that the child becomes aware of his or her social label and then looks out for information about what is expected of people in this category:

> Perhaps children begin to pay particular attention to the same-sex model in a special effort to learn the social rules appropriate for their own sex – that is, to begin to engage in self-socialization. (Slaby and Frey 1975:854)

Sprafkin and Liebert (1978), in an experimental study, where six- to eight-year-old children had the opportunity to choose between male character-focused (*Brady Bunch*) and female character-focused programmes (*Nanny and the Professor*), found that boys preferred the former, and girls the latter. Children in this age range are likely to be at advanced stages of gender constancy, and it is interesting to note that Sprafkin and Liebert found that selective attention towards same-sex characters was highest for those episodes which were most clearly sex typed. This is consistent with McArthur's (1982) claim that selective attention will be directed more to extreme behaviours than to moderate ones (see Chapter 1).

Accounting for sex role information in television

Having seen that children do appear to take the sex of the actor into account in their viewing patterns, the next important question to raise is: what do they make of the sex stereotyped content that these viewing strategies may render accessible? There are various ways to tackle this question and the favoured method of many psychologists is experimental study. A number of relevant experiments will be discussed shortly. A different, though complementary, approach is to *ask* them – that is, to probe children's understanding of sex stereotyped TV material using interview techniques – and we will consider some evidence based on this approach first.

In one such study, a number of young children were invited to discuss four brief segments of sex stereotyped material and to explain some of the actions and motives of the males and females within them (Durkin 1984). The materials were chosen from different types of television broadcasts and a deliberate effort was made to choose instances of stereotypes established as frequent in the content analysis literature (see Chapter 2). They were:

   (i) a clip from the *Superman* film where Superman rescues a
     distressed Lois Lane from a trapped helicopter;
  (ii) a commercial for a deodorant spray called *Impulse*, the
     demonstrable consequence for a beautiful young woman of
     using this toiletry in the morning being that on her way to
     work a handsome young male stranger leaps off a train and
     rushes (impulsively) to buy and present her with a bunch of
     flowers;
 (iii) an excerpt from a children's film about a brave young
     nobleman, *Gawain the Green Knight*, in which the hero rides
     his horse dramatically into a castle, where in the midst of
     melee and danger, a beautiful young maiden appears and
     offers nurturantly to bandage a slight wound he has recently
     sustained; and
 (iv) an excerpt from an educational broadcast called *Going Shopping*, in which a mother, presented as a traditional housewife,
     takes her small son out to town.

The children, who ranged in age from four to nine years, were
interviewed individually, watching the videotaped materials in the
company of a female interviewer. After each segment, they were asked
a series of predetermined questions and any other questions or
clarifications that seemed appropriate in the course of discussion. The
purpose of the work was to uncover preliminary information on the
kinds of social-cognitive processes that children may be capable of
bringing to bear on their TV viewing, such as the inferences they
make, the patterns they detect, the motives they recognize and the
predictions and explanations that they offer. It was assumed, for
reasons indicated in Chapter 3, that these are important aspects of the
ways in which children construct their understanding of the social
world, and that studies of imitation or short-term responses are not
necessarily the best way to begin to study these internal processes (if
they occur).

Children were asked questions such as was Lois frightened? Was
Superman frightened? Why, in the *Impulse* commercial, did the young
man give the young woman flowers? Do ladies wear armour and fight,
like *Gawain*? Where was 'Daddy' while Mummy was *Going Shopping*?

Their responses to these types of questions were clear and consistent. Irrespective of age, virtually all the children knew that Lois was
frightened but Superman was not. They knew that the young man
gave flowers because he 'liked' (some said 'loved') the woman. The
idea of women wearing armour and going off to war was generally
considered amusingly improbable. 'Daddy', it was unanimously
announced, was out 'at work'.

Further questions were used to probe these responses and to coax elaborations. For example, children were asked to imagine a *Super-woman* and to estimate whether she would be able to rescue people in the same way. (This was before the *Superwoman* film had been released.) All of the children felt this was unlikely. They explained that 'men are stronger than ladies' (girl aged 4½) and insisted that this would be the case even if the hypothetical *Superwoman* had superpowers – a good example of the focus on overt, physical differences between the sexes which Ullian (1976) and others have claimed characterize the sex-role conceptualization of children at this early stage. When they had explained that the young man gave flowers because he liked the woman, they were asked to imagine that he liked the train driver, would he give him flowers, too? Most children thought this idea was funny. Similarly, they thought that, if the woman liked the man, she would not be very likely to run after him and give him flowers.

On the *Gawain* excerpt, children were asked what the women would do while the armoured men were out fighting. This was easy: 'Stay at home and do the washing' (girl aged six years, 11 months), 'Tidy up' (girl aged 6½) were typical responses. Conversely, the absent Daddy in *Going Shopping* was expected to be ill-disposed towards housework, and likely to be incompetent at it.

These responses are not especially surprising, but they do tell us some revealing things about young children's implicit grasp of TV material. Note that most of the questions elicit answers that show clear reference to social conventions and to conventional sequences of behaviour. In virtually every case, the child moves easily 'beyond the information given'. Children recognize the emotional states of the characters (fear, liking), they understand the one-way expectations about who gives flowers to whom in our culture, they make ready guesses about the whereabouts of people not visible nor even referred to in the excerpts, and these guesses reveal accurate knowledge of contemporary sex role stereotypes.

Of course, quite how much these children's prior TV viewing has contributed to the development of this knowledge is not revealed by these data. But what the findings do indicate is that children can, apparently without great difficulty, infer relationships, detect themes, and elaborate systematically upon the particular material they view. In other words, they can indeed bring social-cognitive processes to bear on their TV experience. They seem, in fact, to engage in *scriptal* processes, readily providing skeletal accounts of the social settings and interactions with which they were confronted. These accounts enable them to make reference in a logically consistent way to events or persons that they did not actually view. Some of the most interesting properties of their responses are superficially the most obvious: for example, they mention *general* activities that, a cognisant member of

Western culture would know, are stereotypically likely for men in general (like being at work), or women in general (like washing up), but they do not usually call up *specific* or idiosyncratic activities that random guessing or unstructured recall might promote. All of this is consistent with more extensive accounts, concluding that the development of script knowledge in young children 'is general in form, temporally organized, consistent over time and socially accurate' (Nelson 1981:103).

The children's appraisal of the television excerpts is somewhat different from the notion of the child as a passive recipient, accumulating the mass of repetitive images that content analyses have exposed. Two other impressions gleaned from these interviews amplify this point and its implications. First, in the case of the *Going Shopping* material, several children found it quite difficult to disentangle their predictions about family life in the TV setting they had just viewed from their own domestic experiences. They reported on whether their own fathers did the washing up, whether their own mothers went out to work and so on. To state the obvious, this suggests that children may use information from various sources in attempting to understand the world around them – and a good source of information about domestic life is one's own domestic life. While this is only an impressionistic suggestion, and further research which attempted more systematically to contrast home knowledge with TV images would be valuable, it does tie in with other theoretical and empirical considerations (to which we return in Chapter 7), and with common sense.

Secondly, a couple of children made remarks which indicated some incipient meta-awareness of the ways in which TV presents social information. For example, one seven-year-old girl mentioned that 'you usually don't have women when they're fighting', and one six-year-old boy explained that women do not wear armour because, 'Well, on films I see she don't wear anything; only her dress'. Notice that the topics here concern psychologically *distant* events, such as war apparel in ancient times, rather than domestic matters on which the child has other information. Again, these are merely anecdotal observations which call for more research, but they do illustrate the possibility that children of this age can detect some broad patterns in television material.

Recognizing sex stereotyped features of television

More substantial evidence on this possibility comes from a study by Huston *et al.* (1984), investigating children's understanding of the

sex-linked associations of the *formal* features of television. Welch *et al.*
(1979) had already shown (as discussed in Chapter 2) that the visual
techniques and sound track of TV commercials varied substantially
according to whether the product was intended for boys and girls. In
the more recent investigation, Huston *et al.* (1984) asked: can children
themselves detect these subtle background variations? In a careful
experiment, they presented children aged approximately six to 12
years with a series of authentic or artificial commercials and tested
their awareness of whether a particular style of presentation would be
appropriate to advertise a boy's toy or a girls' toy. Similarly, some
children were given a verbal description questionnaire in which they
had to decide which formal features would be appropriate to advertising a sex typed toy. The features included having the toy move
around a lot, having loud, fast music, having men talk about the toy,
versus using a lot of 'fades', having a woman talk about the toy, and
having soft, quiet music. For the adult familiar with a Western TV
culture it is obvious that if the product was a toy truck, the first three
of these features would be most appropriate, according to sex
stereotyped expectations, than the latter three, while the reverse
would apply if the product were a toy pram. How obvious is this to six-
to 12-year-old viewers?

The results showed that even the youngest subjects were quite
good at identifying these sex stereotyped features of ads. Older
children were more accurate than younger, but all age groups tested
showed significant understanding of these properties of TV. This
work points to important issues for future research concerning the
nature of 'media literacy' in children, and its relationship to the
development of social understanding. For the moment, it contributes
further evidence that children's involvement with TV is not randomly
absorptive but calls upon their abilities to detect structure and
associations in complex stimuli.

By around eight years, children are able to rate the stereotypically
male or female characteristics of TV characters, and it appears that
their ratings are accurate (or at least that they coincide with what
adult investigators perceive in the same content). Mayes and Valentine (1979) had eight- to 13-year-old children rate the extent to which
they perceived cartoon characters to possess personality attributes
derived from Rosenkrantz *et al.* (1968) and Bem (1974). The attributes were rephrased in terms which could reasonably be expected to
be comprehensible to children in this age range. The findings show
marked differences in the rated properties according to sex of character. Male characters were likely to be rated as *brave, dominant, leaderlike*
and so on, while female characters were rated low on these attributes.
This was the case irrespective of sex of subject.

Unfortunately, Mayes and Valentine chose sex typed personality attributes which are almost all positively associated with masculinity, while femininity is defined by their absence. (This is not inevitable, as there are stereotypically feminine characteristics for which the reverse applies.) This may mean that the study had demand characteristics (built-in methodological features that provide the subject with cues to what is expected of him/her) that exaggerated the strength of some of the findings. The children may have recognized that the words (such as 'brave') denoted male characteristics and thus *expected* to find them in the male figures but not in the females (a general problem in content analytic work in this area; see Chapter 2). Nevertheless, the findings are interesting and compatible with the broad argument here that children may use their existing knowledge when viewing new material.

The extent to which children of different ages are able to recognize and interpret sex related characteristics in television content is interesting, but of course there is more to the story than 'cold' cognitive appraisal. Important questions are, to what extent do children *identify* with TV characters, to what extent do they *imitate* them, and under what conditions are they consciously *influenced by* them?

These are core questions about television influence that have attracted attention in connection with neighbouring topics, especially violence. They are also questions to which the answer often seems obvious to the layperson. Yet the answers are not always clear-cut even in areas of television effects that have been extensively investigated and, with respect to sex roles, the little research that is available does not provide an exhaustive or conclusive account, as we will see in the following sections.

Identifying with TV personalities

Miller and Reeves (1976), for example, conducted an interesting study of third to fifth grade children's identifications with TV characters. Given the evidence of over-representation and higher status of males in TV, they expected to find that boys would nominate more televised models than would girls, and that boys would nominate more same-sex characters than would girls. In fact, they found that only slightly over half of the children nominated *any character at all* with whom they identified. Boys named more models than girls, but the means were low (0·81 for boys, 0·57 for girls). Clearly, this does not point to obsessive preoccupations with TV models. Boys did nominate only male characters, while 27% of the girls who did nominate any character specified males.

This latter finding can be interpreted in various ways. On the one hand, a small proportion of the female population in this age range could be identifying with cross-sex TV models because of the scarcity of same-sex representatives. On the other hand, a larger proportion have either found a same-sex model to identify with, despite these odds, or have not identified with *any* TV model. Whether it is a good or a bad thing to identify with a same-sex TV model is another (important) issue, which was not the direct concern of the study. Perhaps a larger proportion of girls do not identify with TV models because they find them trivial or unrealistic. One further possibility is that among the 27% of the girls who expressed identification with opposite sex characters was a high proportion of pubertal children experiencing sexual attraction to glamorous TV stars, and their express desire to 'be like' these men could relate to social fantasies, such as joining the media jet set. Boys lag behind agemate girls in the onset of puberty (Tanner 1972) and it may be less likely that these male children would express corresponding desires yet. But note that one could invert this argument: maybe the 27% were largely 'tom-boyish' girls who had not yet experienced the menarche and were much less concerned about traditional femininity than their peers. Finally, the fact that boys only mentioned male figures should not of course be attributed exclusively to the effects of medium bias. Sex role development in boys is more rigid and allows less scope for cross-sex behaviour (Brooks-Gunn and Matthews 1979; Archer 1984). It is conceivable that boys would be reluctant to admit to identification with female figures even if they experienced it.

These are not criticisms of Miller and Reeves' study, but indications that the findings are open to several interpretations. Similar observations can be made of another creative investigation by the same researchers in which children (of roughly the same age range as the 1976 study) were asked to make similarity judgements between all possible pairs of 15 concepts, where the concepts were the names of 14 familiar TV characters and the self ('me'). This is an intuitively attractive measure of identification, eliciting the child's subjective perceptions of personal distance to the TV models. In this study (Reeves and Miller 1978), the authors again expected to find that boys would identify more with TV characters, especially same-sex ones, while girls would be more likely to identify with male TV characters than boys would with female characters.

Unfortunately, Reeves and Miller were faced with a problem that is not surprising in the light of the content analysis findings (Chapter 2): they could not find enough female targets in current TV characters to achieve a balanced experimental design. Thus, of the 14 characters they chose as potential identification figures, only three were female.

This sets problems for the interpretation of their results. The main problem is that they actually found no significant difference between boys and girls on the measure of identification with the opposite sex. This suggests that girls *do* identify with the limited numbers of female stars made available. (Reeves and Miller interpret their results slightly differently; see Durkin (1985b) for a fuller discussion of the details.)

Howitt and Cumberbatch (1976), in a study of how much British adolescent children felt they would wish 'to be like' a number of TV and real-life models, found that 11- to 15-year-old girls did indeed express greater desires than boys to resemble female pop singers who appeared frequently on TV. This study revealed several groupings of media personalities with whom different children identified to different extents. There were some sex differences, in that girls seemed to like the roles of *Coronation Street* characters more than boys, while boys expressed greater interest in being like sports commentators, but there were no sex differences in several areas, including aspirations to the roles of aggressive heroes. Note that in all of these cases, the data are only *suggestive* of the reasons why such orientations are experienced. There may be hidden sex differences concerning which aspects of the characters' appeal to the viewers: it could be that boys like aggressive heroes because they dominate people, while girls like them because they use their skills to resolve problems and redress iniquities. Most likely, of course, there are individual differences *within* sex in this respect, and many young viewers will have complex rather than single-factor reasons for liking specific characters. Finally, note too that responses to a questionnaire which tests your desire to be like such notables as *Bob Monkhouse*, *Dr. Who*, *Elsie Tanner* and *Captain Kirk*, may well reveal interesting facets of your personality but do not directly expose the extent to which these aspirations govern your everyday reasoning and behaviour.

Identification studies, still few and far between in this area, are important because they hint at the ways in which young viewers discriminate among, and attach values to, familiar TV characters, and thus begin to probe the *affective* components of the viewer–medium relationship. We noted in Chapter 3 that affect is strongly involved in sex role development, and the relationship between this aspect of self and the processing of TV images calls for more extensive study. At present, we can conclude that the relationship is interesting but not exhaustively investigated, and that it is clearly more intricate than an exclusive identification between viewer and same-sex stars.

Imitation of TV characters

Do children imitate same-sex TV characters? As suggested earlier, lay opinion often seems to affirm that they do. Occasional tragic

stories of little boys emulating *Batman* and leaping from bedroom
windows, or cute anecdotes of precocious girls borrowing make-up
and tights in order to dress like some movie goddess, provide vivid
instances of such behaviour. Most parents and primary school
teachers will confirm that children do borrow from and enact TV
scripts in their play (see, e.g. Lyle and Hoffman 1976; Singer and
Singer 1981). But such evidence does not really indicate how pervasive such imitation may be, nor whether children derive patterns of
behaviour and beliefs from such play that carry over into their
non-play behaviour and development. It may be diverting to be
Mr Spock for half an hour before dinner, but you would not necessarily aspire to life-long pointed ears because of this transient
identification.

According to Social Learning Theory, differential imitation of
same-sex models is an early and fundamental step in sex role development, laying the groundwork for the later establishment of sex role
identity. In fact, the evidence on same-sex imitation is mixed and it is
clear that other factors are involved, making the relationship between
child and modelled behaviour much more complex than we might at
first expect. Barkley *et al.* (1977), for example, summarize a review of
81 studies testing the 'same-sex hypothesis' that children will display
greater imitation of the same-sex model. Only 18 of these provided
evidence in support of the hypothesis.

What factors influence whether a child will imitate a same-sex
model? Barkley *et al.* argued that the sex typing of the modelled
behaviour and its appropriateness for the sex of the observer might be
more important than simply the sex of the model or the observer. To
test this, they presented seven-year-old children with videotaped
male or female models playing with toys which had been predetermined to be sex typed. Thus, a male actor was seen playing with
masculine toys *or* with feminine toys, and so on. After viewing, the
children were observed while playing with the same toys. The results
revealed that girls imitated modelled feminine behaviour more than
boys, irrespective of the sex of the model displaying the feminine
behaviour. The pattern of results for boys was similar but did not
reach statistical significance (an outcome which the authors attribute
to the special attractiveness of one of the toys which the boys seemed
to like playing with irrespective of the experimental condition to
which they had been allocated). This work suggests that children impose their pre-existing schema of sex appropriate behaviour
upon their viewing and adapt their own 'imitative' behaviour ac-
cordingly. Thus modelling follows understanding, rather than the
reverse.

The influence of verbal information

Masters *et al.* (1979) extended the findings of Barkley *et al.* (1977) in important ways by contrasting two possible sources of information about the sex appropriateness of a particular behaviour: the sex of the model and a sex-appropriateness verbal label. They adopted a similar experimental procedure to that of Barkley *et al.* but used toys which had been shown in pretesting to be neutral with respect to sextyping. Thus, in their design there was less likelihood of pre-existing toy preferences influencing the children's play. The subjects were aged four to five years.

Masters *et al.* found that there was no direct effect of the *model's* sex upon children's imitation of preference, but that there was a strong tendency for children to adopt or express a preference for behaviour that was labelled in the videotapes as appropriate to their sex. Labels appeared to have what the authors call 'dual power': they increase children's play with 'sex appropriate' toys, and decrease their willingness to play with opposite sex toys.

Sex of model was related to sex labelling in interesting ways in Masters *et al.*'s findings. When a toy labelled as sex-inappropriate was played with by a model of the same sex as the child, then the child was less likely to avoid the toy than a child who had seen it manipulated by an opposite-sex model. Presumably, the evidence of a same-sex person playing with the dubious plaything made it less objectionable to the young viewer. Most interesting of all, though, was the surprising finding that children who viewed toys labelled as sex-appropriate but played with by opposite-sex models were the most likely group to choose the modelled toys. Masters *et al.* suggest that children infer that, if the toy is so good that an opposite-sex person is prepared to violate norms to play with it, then it must be especially attractive. It seems, then, that explicit messages can influence a child's willingness to imitate sex typed behaviours that he or she sees on screen, though this factor can interact with others such as sex of actor.

Another study demonstrating an effect upon children's toy preferences due to verbal message is an investigation by Cobb *et al.* (1982). They had *Muppets* present stereotyped reasons why a given set of toys belonged (in different experimental conditions) to a boy, to a girl, or to children of both sexes. The materials were selected because they were found in pilot work to be chosen for play equally often by boys and girls, but in the films the *Muppets* explained that they knew they were a boy's because you could throw or punch them, or a girl's because you could rock or hug them, and so on. After viewing, the children had an opportunity to play with the toys seen in the film as well as a set of comparison toys, known to be less attractive to children of the age range tested (four- to six-year-olds). There were quite strong effects due to condition in this experiment, with children spending more time playing with the toys defined as sex-appropriate. Children who had seen toys defined as sex-inappropriate spent more time playing with the less appealing comparison toys.

It is worth noting that even in the sex-inappropriate conditions, the children did spend some time (approximately 4 out of 10 minutes) playing with the 'prohibited' toys. It may be that these were the latter minutes of the observation period – perhaps the children soon grew tired of the boring toys and managed to overcome their sex role constraints in the interests of more fun. Nevertheless, combined with similar results in the Masters *et al.* experiment, these findings have important implications for the study of young children's responses to TV messages. Some areas of real TV do convey fairly overt indications of sex appropriateness, and as we have seen, commercials (including, of course, toy commercials) are particularly salient examples.

Commercial messages

Ruble *et al.* (1981) investigated the effects on children's sex role behaviour and beliefs of viewing televised toy commercials which presented *either* two boys *or* two girls playing with the target toy. Pretesting had shown the toy to be gender-neutral (i.e. not associated by children with one sex or the other). As in the Slaby and Frey (1975) study discussed earlier the children, aged three to six years, were administered a measure of gender constancy and classified on the basis of responses to this as at high or low gender stages. Ruble *et al.* found that a single viewing of the commercial had considerable impact upon the children's inclination to play spontaneously with the toy when they had an opportunity to do so, but only among those children who were at the high gender stage. Compared to children in a control condition who saw no commercials, high gender stage children were much more likely to spend time playing with the toy when it was presented as sex-appropriate, and much less likely to do so when it was associated with the opposite sex. High gender stage children were also more likely to reply, when questioned, that the toy was inappropriate for members of their own sex, if they had seen it demonstrated by opposite sex figures in the commercial. Since Ruble *et al.* did not rely on an explicit (verbal) message about sex appropriateness, it is interesting to speculate on whether Cobb *et al.* (1982) managed to influence even some of their subjects at lower levels of gender constancy by drawing attention directly to labels. The interaction of gender knowledge and language in such contexts remains to

be tested, and poses important questions for future research into the
ways in which messages are most effectively conveyed in children's
television.

One other investigation provides additional evidence on the
effects of sex role messages in TV commercials, but this time among
an audience of adolescent females. Tan (1979) presented 16- to
18-year-old American high school girls with 15 network TV beauty
commercials in one sitting, and contrasted their post-viewing attitudes to the importance of beauty with those of a comparable group of
girls who saw 15 other commercials which did not mention beauty
themes. The girls who saw the beauty ads rated the importance of
beauty greater than the other group, with respect to 'popularity with
men', though no significant differences emerged on evaluations of the
importance of beauty in career success or success as a wife. There was
also a tendency for girls in the 'beauty' group to rate beauty as
'personally desirable' (to themselves) more highly than the girls who
saw the other ads, though this did not reach statistical significance.
The 'beauty' group recalled more of the products represented in their
ads than the control group did, but rated them as less effective in
persuading others to buy the product.

Since the control ads included such products as dog food, soy
sauce, and three types of disposable diapers, it is not surprising that a
group of adolescents found them only moderately memorable. What
is particularly interesting about this experiment, though, is the effect
on the measure of beauty as important to popularity with men.
Obviously, these were unlikely to be the first beauty commercials the
girls would have seen, and it is reasonable to assume that by this age,
physical attractiveness would be an issue on which most adolescents
would have an opinion, yet the saturated dose of 15 ads seemed to
have at least a short-term effect of intensifying an attitude about the
importance of stereotyped feminine appearance.

It is worth stressing that this is, of course, very much the 'message'
of the ads, and even if not explicitly stated it is inevitably rendered
pretty transparent by the nature of the commercial genre. Hence, this
interesting evidence of short-term effect due to an unusually high
exposure to a particular type of TV content should not be overstated.
Research is also needed to discover the effects of more covert elements
of sex stereotyping in TV – and that research has not yet been
undertaken on a large scale.

It should also be stressed that we are talking of 'effects' here in the
rather formal sense of a demonstrable difference in subjects' response
according to experimental manipulations. This does not mean that
the ads 'caused' a belief that beauty was important in assuring
popularity with males. More likely it reminded these girls of information they had already acquired, and it may have prompted them to

attach particular importance to that information briefly. In the same way, most of us may have a working conviction that war is a bad thing, and find that TV coverage of say, the Falklands, causes a short-term intensification of our feelings. This does not necessarily mean that TV causes us to dislike war. What may be happening when we view news of the Falklands, or beauty or toy commercials, or even disposable diaper recommendations, is that the TV is making phenomena available to our consciousness which we process and assess with reference to a complex and organized set of knowledge and values that we have already acquired.

Watching and seeing

Much of popular and academic thinking about children and television has been dominated by notions of the child 'glued to the box', mindlessly absorbing the (often undesirable) images and messages that the TV companies opt to transmit. According to this view, the child plays a minimal role in the acquisition of values and information, and instead is gratuitously 'shaped' or 'conditioned' by the perpetrators of violence, sexuality, sexism and so on at TV headquarters. There has never really been much research evidence to support this simplified conception (see Anderson and Lorch (1983) for a wider discussion), but its intuitive appeal, and its coincidence with the everyday observation that TV viewing certainly does *look like* passive behaviour, have led to its widespread acceptance.

In this chapter, we have reviewed evidence which is consistent with a rather different conception of children as active viewers, attending selectively to aspects of TV content and using them to check hypotheses, gather new information and impose interpretations upon them which reflect broader dimensions of their attempts to understand the social world, in particular their developing awareness of the importance and durability of gender categories. We find that they are able to call upon their understanding of routines of sex role behaviour – their social scripts – and to use this to explain stereotyped incidents in TV material. Indeed, they sometimes find it difficult to avoid doing so, and move 'back and forth' (Winick and Winick 1979) from accounts of television events to those of their home life.

There are many gaps in our knowledge of how children interpret and evaluate social information in TV, but the evidence available to date does support the view that the processes are active and constructive, both in general and in respect of our specific topic in this book. It seems that the more the child watches, the more it sees, in that it develops competencies as a social being and as a viewer which enable

it better to attend and respond to information and influence presented
in TV. Recognizing that these processes are basic to the viewer–
medium relationship is an important step towards an account which
is both *developmental* and *social*, as introduced in Chapter 3.

A developmental perspective is needed to acknowledge the fundamental importance of the child's abilities and limitations which
determine the use it makes of TV content. This awareness contributes
simultaneously to a social perspective on the 'effective diffusion of
ideas and stereotypes' that we saw in Chapter 1 to be a central interest
for the social psychologist. In contrast to theories of *uni*directional
influence, such as the biological and environmental approaches, it is
suggested here that the information made available by the 'sender',
and presumably consistent with some narrow range of world views
endorsed by the medium, is potentially available to the 'receiver' to
interpret (or discount) in accord with her or his social-cognitive
attainments and needs. These vary at different points in the lifespan and in different individuals in different situations (we return
to these issues in Chapter 7), and realizing this vitiates casual
assumptions that TV acts upon all children the same way, as
a kind of nasty injection that accumulates in their intellectual
bloodstreams.

It is important to recognize that the distinction between superficially attractive metaphors of media effects, such as injections and
conditioning (see Chapter 1), and a social-cognitive approach is more
than a matter of academic delicacy. If children are actively involved
in the transmission and perpetuation of negative social stereotypes by
virtue of their readiness to scour the environment for data relevant to
their personal development, then the processes may be not only more
complex than some accounts maintain, but also more powerful. We
have found hints, for example, in some of the work reviewed in this
chapter that young children attend particularly to extreme or clear-
cut (including explicitly labelled) examples of sex role behaviour, and
that they have strong expectations about sex roles with which these
elements in TV are compatible. In short, maintaining naive effects
models may foster oversimplifications which impede our understanding of the problem and undermine our prospects for discovering the
solution.

We return to some of the broader issues in Chapter 7. Before that,
however, we need to take up more directly the topic of 'solution'.
Television is a medium which can *in principle* be exploited to convey
any message, and it is possible to use it to present children with
counterstereotyped images and themes concerning sex role behaviour. This offers additional ways of examining conceivable
effects and has obvious practical interest to anyone concerned
with the prospects for social change in this area of human affairs.

We turn in the next chapter, therefore, to research investigating the impact upon children of non-traditional sex role portrayals in television.

SIX

Changing the message: children's reactions to counterstereotyped sex role themes in television

Contemporary society has evolved rather ambiguous patterns of attitudes and behaviour towards television. Almost every home has one and almost everybody watches it from time to time. Yet we exercise vigorously our rights to criticize it, if not actually to turn it off, and we worry regularly about its harmful effects (upon others). Research has reflected these preoccupations: television, as the primary mass medium, is seen as an important focus for investigation, and much of the investigation concentrates, reasonably enough, on its potentially harmful effects (upon others). The research question has more often been 'what is wrong with television' rather than 'what is, or could be, right' (Dorr Leifer *et al.* 1974).

But of course television content could be changed. It could be altered to reflect different people's views of what is 'right', and many individuals and organizations both inside and outside the medium have campaigned for changes in the way TV represents the sexes. We have seen, in Chapter 2, that their efforts may be having some modest consequences here and there, though the available evidence on recent developments suggests that things have some way to go before the representations of the sexes could sensibly be called balanced and non-sexist. Quite obviously, the prospects for continuing improvements in TV sex role content are related to broader socio-political considerations. For that reason, much of this chapter will be devoted to changes *in principle* rather than in practice.

We will be considering here a number of experiments and field studies which have attempted to investigate the effects of changing television sex role content, so as to portray the sexes in a more equal light and to demonstrate the possibilities for individuals to engage in activities and life-styles that incorporate behaviour traditionally associated with the opposite sex. In short, we will be concerned with the possible use of TV to transmit counterstereotyped images.

This topic raises a number of interesting questions – ideological, psychological and ethical. The ideological issues include such matters as why has the notion of 'counterstereotyping' emerged at this particular point in social history, and what prospects are there for authentic attempts to develop counterstereotyped media in contemporary societies which still rest upon sexual divisions of labour? Serious treatment of these issues would be scope for another book, and would need to draw upon quite distinct fields of enquiry from that represented in the present account. For our purposes it will be useful to bear in mind the obvious, that interest in 'counterstereotyping' is part of the contemporary re-examination of sex roles among the Western middle-classes, and that the interest is not shared unanimously among the people in power in our societies. The practical consequence of this, I think, is that actual attempts to increase the broadcasting of counterstereotyped material will be met by controversy through the foreseeable future. For this reason and others it is essential to know what the effects of such material may be.

The discussion here will therefore be given to an examination of the social psychological issues: specifically, what happens when an audience is presented with counterstereotyped television images? First, I will consider some of the theoretical issues bearing upon what effects we could expect counterstereotyped material to have on young viewers, then I will go on to review the limited but growing amount of empirical evidence. This evidence reveals mixed outcomes: sometimes counterstereotyping work seems to fail, and sometimes it seems to have the desired effect. The conditions that appear to determine the success or otherwise of such interventions in social understanding will be examined, and finally I will discuss some of the ethical and practical issues at stake in this type of work.

Switch channel, switch society?

Perhaps the most obvious, and certainly the most optimistic, prediction we could make about the effects of presenting young people with
counterstereotyped sex role messages is that the experience will lead
to a redirection of the children's sex role beliefs and attitudes towards
a more egalitarian and less restrictive world view. At its simplest, the
idea here might be that, by changing the dose or by refashioning the
mould, we can change the course of children's development. There
are at least two major problems with this assumption. First, it sustains
the misconception that social and cognitive development can be
explained primarily in terms of external forces; we have already seen
sufficient difficulties for this perspective and need not review them
again. Secondly, it overlooks the fact that even the ubiquitous and
popular TV set cannot be taken as a socializing agent independent
of all others: changes in TV content need at the very least to be
assessed in relation to constancies and changes elsewhere in the social
environment.

Few researchers or broadcasters working on counterstereotyping
in TV suppose that their work can single-handedly predetermine a
new and better world. This amounts to an attribution of omnipotence
to the medium that is an unrealistic as it is undesirable. It is most
unlikely that we can change the structures and values of a society as
easily as we can change channels on a TV set. There are, none the less,
specifiable goals to such interventions which may be more interesting
at the theoretical level and more justifiable at the practical level.

First, it may be possible to encourage the development of more
accurate conceptions of human potential than those encapsulated in
mass media stereotypes. There is nothing psychologically irreverent
in supposing that children can acquire and accommodate new information, and many societies devote whole sectors of their organizational structures to the systematic pursuit of such advances – our
educational systems. In the present context, it is compatible with
most theories of learning that the child could acquire new data about
possible behaviours of female and male people.

Secondly, in so far as new information may well conflict with 'old'
information congruent with social stereotypes, then this context may
provide variously on obstacle to recognition and acceptance *or* a
backdrop against which the non-traditional idea or person could
appear especially salient. In other words, pre-existing learning and
expectations may block the child's perception and evaluation of
counterstereotyped ideas, or alternatively:

> One could argue that the very pervasiveness of traditional sex roles
> in television may be the basis of their undoing. The presentation of

> nontraditional sex roles might have high information value and
> attract the attention of the audience. (Williams *et al.* 1981:30)

We will consider these possibilities further as we review the evidence
from studies exploiting counterstereotyped TV content.

One other preliminary point which must be stressed is that
evidence that viewing counterstereotyped material can lead to
changes in children's attitudes is *not* in itself evidence that viewing
traditional sex stereotyped material has led to the establishment of
those attitudes in the first place. This is sometimes inferred in reviews
of this topic but rests on a false analogy. TV sex role stereotypes,
which the child watches in indisputably large amounts, are broadly
consistent with a host of other potential influences and, however we
characterize the developmental processes at stake in these contexts, it
is clear that they are occurring throughout the child's social life most
of the time. A counterstereotyped message, on the other hand,
contradicts the normal flow of information and behaviour, and thus
offers a radically different learning experience. Acquiring a script in
the first place and responding to violations of it in the second cannot
be assumed to be identical processes.

Watching versus seeing counterstereotypes

As we have considered in earlier chapters, children's use of television
appears to be an active and selective business which functions in
relation to the child's developing social-cognitive skills, interests,
beliefs and motivations. The same complex and often covert factors
need to be taken into account in attempting to understand children's
responses to counterstereotypes.

A striking example of this is provided by a group of studies by
Drabman and colleagues, which attempted to broaden young children's knowledge of which sex could be a doctor or nurse. Each of
these occupations is strongly identified with a specific sex in many
cultures, and Drabman *et al.* (1981) attempted to persuade children
that both career roles could actually be occupied by men or women,
by showing them role-reversal videotaped films. The films presented
a male nurse and a female doctor and emphasized their occupation
and their gender. For example, stress was placed on their names,
which were chosen to heighten the saliency of sex, and their professional titles (e.g. 'Dr Mary Nancy' and 'Nurse David Gregory'). After
viewing, the children were tested and their recall of the sex of the
doctor and nurse, either by recognizing the name or by identifying
among photographs.

The results showed that children tended to 'reverse back' the
gender of the actors, so that the male was identified as a doctor and the

female as a nurse. In similar work, Cordua *et al.* (1979) obtained
compatible results, and also found a stronger tendency to misidentify
the male nurse as a doctor than to misidentify the female doctor as a
nurse. Cordua *et al.* point out that children may well have had direct
experience of female doctors. They conclude that one of the most
difficult tasks for counterstereotyping work may be to dissuade
children of their beliefs about male roles, a point to which we will
return.

The main findings of these experiments are important because
they confirm that, as suggested above, young children may 'watch'
counterstereotyped portrayals without 'seeing' the point. Perception
is not isomorphic with television content. Also interesting is the result
that although *teenage* children did correctly identify the sex of the
doctor and nurse immediately after viewing, on a test a week later
even they were unable to remember the correct sex (Drabman *et al.*
1981). Their memory, Drabman *et al.* suggest, may have adjusted in
line with the most powerful sex role expectations they normally
maintain.

One powerful sex role expectation for some children may be that
males in TV are more authoritative. Children would certainly have
plenty of evidence for this hypothesis from the general bias in status
allocation between the sexes that we discussed in Chapter 2. What
happens, then, when young viewers are presented with a counterstereotype instance of a woman presenting information auth-
oritatively? An example of this would be newsreading, a traditionally
male role in TV which, as noted in Chapter 2, became increasingly
available to females during the 1970s. Tan *et al.* (1980) found that
although children (aged around eight to 12 years) were uninfluenced
by a newsreader's sex when rating her or him on *believability*, girls
seemed to retain more information presented by a male than by a
female (boys were unaffected by this contrast). Tan *et al.* suggest that
the girls may perceive the male as more powerful and more knowl-
edgeable, and thus be inclined to attend to him more carefully.

So, it seems that simply switching the content is not a guaranteed
mechanism for introducing young children effectively to non-
traditional conceptions of male and female roles. A couple of other
studies amplify this point.

In one relevant experiment, O'Bryant and Corder-Bolz (1978)
showed six- to 10-year-old children a number of commercials in which
actresses were shown in traditionally male jobs (e.g. pharmacist,
welder, butcher, labourer). This manipulation did *not* lead to significant reductions in the traditional stereotyping of occupations by
the young viewers, although the girls who saw woman in traditionally
male jobs did increase their reported *preference* for such employment.
The authors point out that it may be difficult by this means alone to

persuade children that the real world has changed, though it may be possible to stimulate them to reassess some of their attitudes and aspirations.

Of course, six- to 10-year-olds are some way from the job market and unlikely to have particularly realistic conceptions of careers. By early adolescence, such concepts should be somewhat more sophisticated, and more meaningful to the child. What prospects do counterstereotyped career films have with this age range?

Durkin and Hutchins (1984) attempted to find out by preparing a set of careers tapes which were shown to 12- to 13-year-old pupils in a London comprehensive school. We supposed that one important consideration for producers of such materials could be the mode of presentation of the persuasive message. For example, non-traditional career roles could be *modelled* by showing a person involved in the occupation who just happens to be the opposite sex to that associated with the job. Alternatively, a *reasoned* case could be made for the role reversal, in which the non-traditional worker could explain why *he* chose to become a secretary and *she* opted for plumbing, and they could exhort other young people to consider the same possibilities.

We predicted that a film exploiting the latter technique should be more likely to have an impact upon young adolescents' views of career opportunities because it provides a direct invitation to consider hypothetical alternatives, and thus engages the emerging intellectual powers of this age group. We prepared three versions of a careers film to test this hypothesis, using the same actors and presenter. In one version, the *Traditional* programme, the actors were allocated occupations traditionally associated with their sex (doctor, nurse, plumber, secretary) and in the course of individual interviews explained what the entry qualifications were for the job, what they liked about it, what their long-term prospects were, etc. The other two versions were counterstereotyped. In one, the *Modelling* programme, the actors outlined the same factual information, but just happened to be the opposite sex to that traditionally associated with the role; no explicit attention was given to their unusual status in this respect. In the *Explicit* version, the actors were presented in pairs, so that a male and a female secretary were interviewed simultaneously, and so on through the other occupations; in this version, after the factual discussion, the presenter focused directly upon the role-reversal person and asked, for example, how he felt about being a secretary in a female dominated occupation, or how she got on with male plumbers, and so on. The actors responded in a positive fashion about their work, declaring that they enjoyed it, that they never experienced more than mild mickey-taking from their workmates, that they were soon accepted into the job, and that they would recommend it seriously to other young people of their sex.

The programmes were presented to groups of children as trial careers films which were being tested for their technical quality and general usefulness to pupils thinking about future occupations. Ostensibly, the pupils task was to evaluate the films for this purpose. After viewing the films, the children were given questionnaires which included items designed to lend credibility to this explanation, but which also addressed their general career interests. A fourth group of children were included as controls; they saw no programme but received a modified version of the questionnaire.

The results were reasonably straightforward. All four groups gave strongly traditional responses to the careers questionnaire. This was so for the occupations shown in the films as well as for others not shown but known to be traditionally sex typed (e.g. motor mechanic, nursery teacher). The children identified certain jobs as 'mainly men's work', and others as 'mainly women's work'. Neutral occupations tended to be rated as neutral. To ensure that such responses were not simply a reflection of children's knowledge of actual patterns of employment, we had additional questions asking whether the respondents thought more men *should* be trained to be nurses or more women trained to be plumbers, etc. Again, responses were sex-typed and hostile to non-traditional possibilities, irrespective of programme watched. Indeed there was even some evidence, on male nurses and female doctors, that children who had seen the counterstereotype careers programmes were *more* hostile to change than the other groups.

Of course, we had not expected a complete upheaval of the children's sex role stereotypes and beliefs as a consequence of exposure to one 10-minute fabricated careers programme. Our purpose was to test whether a direct appeal to the young people's reasoning would incur some movement towards acknowledging that certain careers could be opened up to either sex. At least we got a clear answer.

There are, then, obstacles to the detection and acceptance of counterstereotyped sex role messages in TV. Sometimes, children's existing sex role knowledge seems to create such powerful perceptual sets that they simply miss the point. In other cases, they reject non-traditional ideas quite emphatically, and the evidence suggests that they find aversive proposals which would subvert views and values that they have spent several years developing and which relate closely to their personal lives and aspirations. As we have noted in Chapter 3, sex roles *matter*, and young people's feelings and attitudes towards them are not always amenable to intervention.

However, the story does not end there. We turn now to a number of other recent studies which have reported more successful consequences of intervention work.

Counterstereotype experiments that produce significant changes

Flerx *et al.* (1976) were among the first to test the effects upon children of exposure to non-traditional sex role content. They presented five-year-olds with traditional story books, *or* egalitarian books, *or* professionally produced egalitarian films, over a seven-day period. They tested the children before, immediately after and again one week after the intervention period. Both of the experimental groups changed their responses significantly in the direction of egalitarianism on measures of *working mothers, nurturing fathers* and *children's play activities*. Although there was some regression by the time of the final test, the experimental group's responses remained significantly more egalitarian than the control group. The film group was slightly more egalitarian than the book group. Flerx *et al.* also found that boys expressed more stereotyped beliefs than girls and were not as strongly affected as the girls by the egalitarian messages.

Davidson *et al.* (1979) presented three groups of five- to six-year-old girls with cartoon programmes, depicting different levels of sex stereotyping. One group saw a *high* stereotype programme, one saw a *neutral* programme, and the third saw a *reversed* stereotype programme. Afterwards, the girls were administered the Williams *et al.* (1975) Sex Stereotype Measure for children. The girls in the neutral and high stereotype conditions did not differ in their responses, which indicated a moderate level of stereotyping. The girls in the reverse condition, however, gave significantly lower scores (around the midpoint on the scale).

Davidson *et al.* point out that the reverse stereotype cartoon that they used contained overt verbal emphasis on the sex role issues. The programme came from a series called *Kid Power* and entailed a conflict over female rights within a children's clubhouse. The conflict is resolved by sports competitions in which the girls demonstrate unexpected competence. At the end of the episode, a chauvinist piglet concedes that he is glad that girls have been admitted to the club.

This experiment does suggest that counterstereotype messages *can* be grasped by children in this age range, providing they are made sufficiently clear and entertaining. One weakness of the Davidson *et al.* design, which the authors point out, is that because of the low availability of non-traditional materials their programme had to be selected from different series. This means that other aspects of the quality and appeal of the programmes may be confounded with the message. It would also be interesting to contrast children's views before and after viewing the counterstereotyped programme.

Durkin and Akhtar (forthcoming) conducted a comparable investigation with five- to six-year-old English school children, but collected data on children's sex role beliefs before the programmes and again after them. We were fortunate to have available a professionally produced counterstereotype programme from the popular mid-day children's TV series *Rainbow*, and used as a neutral comparison a programme from the same series devoted to the theme of the weather. We also had a third, control group who were exposed to no programme but were tested twice with the same time interval as the other groups. In this way, we could take account of any effects due to re-testing alone, or to simply watching any programme in the company of an experimenter, and contrast children in these experimental conditions with those who saw the counterstereotyped programme.

The counterstereotyping programme was devoted to the theme of role reversal and contained a story about a mother and father changing roles because of unemployment, and various scenes of child care giving by men, constructive work activity by women, and much singing on the theme that most things can be done by either sex (verbal explicitness again). The test was a series of simple questions about who could do various household and occupational tasks, and the child could answer a man, a woman or both. Illustrations of male and female figures were kept in front of the child throughout so that the possible answers were equally evident.

All three groups gave fairly traditional responses on the first test. A week later the role-reversal and the weather groups saw their programmes, and then all three groups were re-tested. The role-reversal group showed significant shifts in the direction of more liberal responses – generally, they gave more 'both' answers. The other groups stayed at the same traditional level, except for girls in the weather group who, unexpectedly, showed a shift in the non-traditional direction too. This may have been due to the fact that the weather programme contained a female who was treated as an equal among males (although no fuss was made about this in the episode). Overall, then, the results were encouraging: non-traditional sex role messages can be understood by children in this age group, and give rise to changed responses on simple tests of sex role beliefs. Of course, the sincerity and durability of those changed responses are not known, and we did not test for modifications in the children's sex role *behaviour*, but this is encouraging evidence that the message can be grasped even by quite young viewers.

Pingree (1978) raised an interesting issue for counterstereotyping research in an experiment with nine- to 15-year-olds in which she gave the children differing accounts of the authenticity of several women depicted in traditional or non-traditional roles in commercials. One group (reality-set) was told the actors were real people, another (acting-set) was told they were actors, and another group was given no information on this matter (no instruction). After viewing, children were given a test of attitudes towards women. Unexpectedly, children who were told they were viewing actors gave less traditional responses than children who were told they were viewing real women – and the type of commercial (traditional or non-traditional) did not affect their responses. Within the reality set group, responses were in line with expectations: the children who viewed traditional ads gave more traditional responses, and viewing the non-traditional ads was associated with less traditional responses.

It could be that being told that the women were actors itself served as a reminder that women can enter glamorous and prestigious occupations. While further work is needed to disentangle these issues, it is worth remembering that as a basis for an intervention technique acting-set information would be somewhat limited. There is probably a fairly low ceiling upon the number of times you can surprise any audience with the news that actors are actors. (Pingree of course is not proposing this.) What is important, if unclear, about these results is the further indication they provide that verbal emphasis and attention directing seem to be related to effects upon viewers.

Another study revealing some non-traditional shifts in children following exposure to TV counterstereotypes is that of McArthur and Eisen (1976). This experiment is important because it attempted to examine the effects of the material upon children's *behaviour*. Children in one condition viewed males displaying nurturance, domesticity and artistic behaviour and females acting bravely, displaying leadership and solving problems. In another condition, children viewed traditional role portrayals. The results showed boys more likely than girls to model their behaviour after a same-sex model, including 'reversal' behaviours. Girls were found to express a significantly greater preference than boys for 'feminine' activities in the stereotyped condition, but not in the reversal condition. The authors conclude that: 'appropriate changes in television's portrayal of the sexes could serve to increase socially desirable, nonstereotyped behaviours on the part of both sexes' (McArthur and Eisen 1976:350). This study, using laboratory produced material, does indeed provide early evidence that such optimism may be supportable, though it is important to note that the range of behaviours at stake and the ages tested are, naturally enough, limited and further research is needed to expand the developmental picture.

The value of experimental studies of
counterstereotyping

One of the obvious limitations upon work of the type described so far in this chapter is that it consists largely of 'single-shot' interventions: the children view as little as *one* programme in some studies, or a few programmes in the space of a quiet short period in others. In the context of the sheer volume of TV exposure that normal children encounter this does appear, in quantitative terms, to be a relative inconsequential experience. However, it would be a mistake to dismiss these experimental findings on the grounds that the real world is a nasty place.

The experimental studies are important for a number of reasons. First, several studies have now shown that the 'messages' of counter-stereotyped material can be transmitted to and grasped by children. Although this does not allow us to conclude that the effects of such novel information will always be the intended ones, it does establish that television can, in principle, offer children a broader view of human potential and that, in some circumstances at least, children will perceive and respond to the message.

Secondly, the work begins to specify under what conditions changes appear to come about (e.g. the age range of the children, the measures used, the nature of the programme, the kinds of emphasis made). Much more needs to be discovered along these lines, but this of course promotes additional experimental studies rather than discounts the few we have.

Thirdly, the possibility that non-traditional messages and images can be recognized by children and taken into account in their responses to sex role tests despite the sheer mass of prior exposure to traditional images, has important implications for intervention studies in the real world.

What amounts to a 'drop in the ocean' effect in laboratory contexts may also occur in the course of natural viewing. Thus, children may sometimes take note of non-traditional behaviour and attitudes as they encounter them, albeit infrequently, in their normal TV use. There is preliminary evidence to support such a speculation: Singer and Singer (1981) found that pre-school girls seem to identify with the more assertive female stars now appearing in U.S. television, such as *Wonder Woman*, *Charlie's Angels*, *Bionic Woman*, and may be emulating some of their behaviours. Fuller tests would be needed to clarify the salience and influence of non-traditional characters encountered in normal viewing, but note that such evidence would bear importantly upon issues discussed earlier in Chapter 4. If children who watch a lot of TV have a greater likelihood of encountering these infrequent images, then this is one factor undermining the expected positive correlation between amount of viewing and degree of sex typing. As we have seen, the expected correlation has not been strong, and this may be part of the reason why.

In sum, the experimental studies do provide important evidence which contributes to the very difficult theoretical and practical tasks of countering traditional sex role stereotypes. This is an area of television research which calls for greater investment of labour.

Nevertheless, the interest and importance of research projects which do include evaluation phases outside the laboratory is obviously equally high. Fortunately, one ambitious venture of this type has already been conducted and has become the subject of two invaluable books in this field. This is the *Freestyle* project, conducted in the United States in the late 1970s, and I conclude my review of the evidence on counterstereotyping with a summary of this intervention experiment.

Outside the laboratory: the Freestyle project

Freestyle was the name of a professionally produced and broadcast 13-part television series designed for nine- to 12-year-olds and intended to convey a variety of counterstereotyped messages in an entertaining format. Each programme lasted for half an hour, and the series focused on a variety of behavioural skills, non-traditional interests and activities, adult work and family roles, all of which were woven into dramatized plots. The principal characters were in the same age range as the target audience, and included girls with mechanical or athletic interests, boys with similar interests and the counterstereotyped abilities to express emotions, engage in nurturant activities, spoof heavily 'macho' images and so on.

The project is a remarkable achievement because of the close collaboration between researchers and professional broadcasters, exploiting a rare opportunity for the fusion of scientific and artistic principles in a mass entertainment context, and because of the scale of the research activity generated in the preparation and evaluation of the programmes. I have reviewed the findings of the research work in greater detail elsewhere (Durkin, 1985c) and will only attempt here to summarize the main results. The two books providing detailed accounts of the development of conceptual and analytical techniques (Williams *et al.* 1981) and the production process and evaluation of the final series (Johnston and Ettema 1982) are essential reading for anyone with a serious interest in counterstereotyping in the mass media.

Among other concerns, Williams *et al.* investigated what children perceived in the counterstereotyped material, and what they liked. They conducted studies with several hundred children and their findings show that responses to the characters vary partly as a function of the sex of the child but also in relation to the sex of the character and the kinds of activities that the character is portrayed in. If the child already had an interest in female-typed activities, for example, then he or she was more likely to like the programme segments containing such activities.

Williams *et al.* found that children's reported desire to model the counterstereotyped characters' behaviours was mixed. Girls modelling intentions were not strongly predicted by variables such as the activities and interests of the characters, while boys' intentions showed some correlation between these and their desire to imitate. Williams *et al.* also found a selective bias in the perception of the programme segments they worked with, such that stereotypical males and non-stereotypical females were more liked and better recalled. There were signs that this was particularly so among boys. The researchers point out that it is possible that this could be due to some undetected variation in the quality of the material, but that it also suggests that 'getting the idea across that men do not have to act stereotypically aggressive (and the like) may be the hardest task of all' (Williams *et al.* 1981:87).

While Williams *et al.* report various tests of comprehension and reaction to excerpts of preparatory materials from *Freestyle*, Johnston and Ettema (1982) describe how the series came into being and provide a detailed account of the effects of viewing the programmes when they were actually broadcast. A total sample of approximately 7000 subjects in several U.S. cities was tested. Children's sex-role beliefs, attitudes and interests were tested before and after the series was broadcast and a sub-sample were given a delayed post-test nine months later.

The children were placed in three different conditions:

   (i) a *viewing/discussion* group in which children watched the programmes at school and then discussed them, led by teachers who had prepared guidelines on the goals of the material;
  (ii) a *viewing/school* group who watched the programmes at school but had no formally organized discussions; and
 (iii) a *viewing/home* group who were simply encouraged to watch the programmes at home when they were broadcast.

The results indicate substantial (though not total) effects in the desired direction in the *viewing/discussion* condition, promoting greater acceptance of (a) girls who engage in athletics and mechanical activities, assume positions of leadership, and display independence,

(b) boys who engage in nurturing activities, and (c) women and men who choose non-traditional careers (Johnston and Ettema 1982:204, Ch. 5). Nine months later, further tests showed some shift away from non-traditional views on some measures but most remained significantly changed from pre-test levels. The target area most resistant to change was found to be beliefs and attitudes concerning childhood *behavioural skills*, particularly relating to girls displaying leaderlike, independent, assertive and risk-taking characteristics. However, Johnston and Ettema point out that these are relatively abstract concepts which are difficult to address directly in a television production. It may be that the (largely pre-adolescent) children failed to detect the relevant themes rather than that they detected them and rejected them. Even so, the possibility remains that the constraints governing perception in this domain are least amenable to modification. One other notion that resisted change was the role of the husband as primary breadwinner – despite various related changes, children persisted in the belief that males support families.

Importantly, the other viewing conditions were less effective. The *viewing/school* condition produced some changes in the same direction to those obtained in the *viewing/discussion* condition, but the strength of the change was not as great, and on serveral measures no change was obtained. The *viewing/home* condition was the least effective. Here the effects were smaller, were limited to outcomes related to girls in mechanics and only obtained among the heaviest viewers of the series (Johnston and Ettema 1982:221). Johnston and Ettema suggest that some of the issues addressed in counterstereotype work call for verbal exchange of ideas before beliefs and attitudes will change. They also point out, though, that children did not appear to be antagonized by the series.

Counterstereotyping: an overview

Several summary points may now be made about the state-of-the-art of research into sex role counterstereotyping in children's TV.

(1) The intended or desired changes do not always materialize; several studies have obtained non-significant results and some have had mixed outcomes. These findings are important because they help to indicate where the main obstacles to counterstereotyping lie. It is worth noting too that the so-called 'file drawer' problem of scientific research – that *non*-significant results are sometimes confused with insignificant results and taken as a sign of the failure of an experiment is likely to have limited the availability of this evidence: researchers are less inclined to submit, and journals are less inclined to publish

negative results. This means that it is difficult to assess the overall balance of the evidence that is published.

(2) Nevertheless, several well-designed experiments have obtained positive results. This indicates that children can understand counter-stereotype messages in some materials, perhaps aided by the distinctiveness that an unusual message attains, and some children do shift their responses on measures of sex role attitudes and behaviours subsequent to viewing.

(3) The durability and resilience of such changes in the face of competing social influences have not been tested extensively, but at least some evidence (Johnston and Ettema 1982) shows that they can be maintained for several months.

(4) While our understanding of what children at different stages of development like and dislike in counterstereotype programmes is fragmentary at present, several studies indicate that positive connotations of power and prestige enhance characters' appeal: an unsurprising finding in the light of much previous research into children and television (Bandura 1977) but nonetheless important because of its reminder to experimenters and broadcasters that their materials must be positive and dynamic to attract the relevant audience. Affective responses to medium messages may be critical to their reception.

(5) Children's concepts of aspects of the traditional male role have been found in several studies to be least amenable to intervention and boys are sometimes less disposed to change their sex role attitudes and beliefs than are girls. This is consistent with the acknowledged rigidity of the traditional male role (Hartley 1959; Archer 1984), and presents an important focus for future research. Some further implications of this point are discussed below, when we turn to ethical and practical considerations.

(6) We have seen evidence in some of the studies reviewed here, echoing points made in Chapter 5, that the *verbal* explicitness of a TV message may influence substantially its reception by young viewers. How to introduce and maintain counterstereotype themes to maximum effect is a central consideration for research and practice, and the verbal dimension stands out as an important focus for future work.

(7) Closely related to this is the evidence from the Johnston and Ettema study that viewing plus discussion proved the most effective condition for the development of non-traditional views. This serves to illustrate two important points: first, that the extent to which the message is articulated and perhaps even debated will influence its impact upon children at least in middle-childhood, and secondly, that

counterstereotyped TV alone will not serve to rectify the social problems of sex role stereotyping and sex role inequality.

Many issues and questions emerge for future enquiry, and research into counterstereotyping is exciting in scope because of its theoretical contributions to our understanding of how social knowledge is organized in childhood and its potential practical contributions to social progress. To stress an earlier point, it would be a delusion to imagine that switching the channel will switch society, but it would be equally facile to decry the experimental and practical work on counterstereotyping because it is not a complete solution.

Ethical and practical considerations in counterstereotyping

So far in this chapter we have largely begged the question of whether we *should* intervene in the sex role development of children by using a popular medium to subvert traditional images. Although the desirability of this kind of work may seem obvious to many interested in the general topic of sex roles, there are in fact a number of ethical and practical issues at stake here, and consideration of these reveals quite substantial problems for researchers, social policy advocates and broadcasters. Considerable caution is always appropriate before engaging in any manipulations that are designed to alter the beliefs and behaviour of other human beings, and the responsibility to exercise this caution is especially great when dealing with children. As we review some of the problems, it becomes clear that launching into a new era of non-traditional TV is a far from straightforward prospect.

Problem 1: Interference in the course of child development

According to some theories of sex role emergence, patterns of development are either predetermined by nature or constructed in regular and predictable sequences. Dabbling in these processes, it could be argued, is potentially obstructive and even harmful. My personal view is that in some circumstances this could well be so. Following a social-cognitive account of sex role acquisition, I have maintained in this book that children construct their social understanding systematically in the course of complex interactions with others. An intervention attempt which disregarded developmental and individual differences in sex role understanding, and contradicted all other aspects of the child's world, could instigate psychosocial discomfort and distress at some points in the early lifespan and may even cause enduring uncertainties for some individuals. Trying to 'cure' six-year-olds of rigid beliefs about sex roles might rob them of naive certainties that help them to see consistency in a complex world.

Problem 2: Lack of unanimity

The good intentions of a group of academic researchers or mass media liberals may not always coincide with the beliefs of the parents of children to whom intervention programmes are addressed. Although many parents resent the flood of sex-stereotyped content their children encounter in TV, the persistence of such fare on our screens indicates that these adults are still in a minority; others may be indifferent or may positively welcome TV's assistance in the transmission of traditional sex role values. Is it justifiable to attempt to countermand parents of the latter persuasion?

Problem 3: Fluctuation of purpose

Good intentions can be subject to shifts in fashion and reassessments of the evidence. A little of both seem to have occurred, for example, in the demise of 'androgyny', which was a very popular idea in the mid-1970s but has been largely abandoned, at least as a goal in life, by the mid-1980s. Androgyny was originally a technical concept in personality theory, which was intended to denote those individuals of either sex whose self-reports indicate that they possess above-median levels of certain traits which are stereotypically masculine and of those which are stereotypically feminine. This rather tentative psychometric notation provides a useful concept for researchers in personality structure but it was rapidly incorporated into the ideological arena where it tended to be heralded as a new standard of healthy and liberated personal adjustment. The suggestion that androgynous people had the 'best of both worlds' led in turn to its adoption in the popular media where the term came to be used interchangeably with 'unisex' and even 'bisexual'. The media themselves now regularly prefix the names of such entertainers as *Michael Jackson*, *Annie Lennox* and *Boy George* with the adjective 'androgynous', seemingly associating anything from unusual vocal quality and unconventional length of hair to outright transvestism with this illustrious property – a far cry from the sombre pages of the *Journal of Consulting and Clinical Psychology* where the term was innocently introduced (Bem 1974). The difficulty with such ephemeral and easily misconstrued popularization of scientific terminology is of course that it may be quite reckless to decide for a particular age cohort of children that they should become 'androgynous' when the criteria for the attainment of this state are constantly shifting and the long-term benefits of pursuing it are unknown. The short history of androgyny is merely an example of a general difficulty here of deciding what constitutes a more desirable social order and how to fit people in to it.

Problem 4: Progress and reaction

Attempts to promote counterstereotyped appeals in TV could have unintended effects, contrary to the actual goals of the broadcasts. Children are well-known to demonstrate psychological reactance to some attempts to direct or influence them. It is easy to see the potential for a regular prosocial message about equality of the sexes to be regarded as the equivalent of a religious broadcast by many young viewers, and thus incur rejection or deliberate opposition. Similarly, attempts in one area of the mass media to alter sex role portrayals stand a good chance of exciting the sensibilities of other professionals who find tradition less objectionable; the latter may be inspired to *increase* their contributions to the perpetuation of sex role stereotypes.

Problem 5: Destructive messages

One of the most difficult considerations in counterstereotyping reflects the inherent fact that any movement for social change must logically be accompanied by some negativity about the existing state of affairs. Individuals or groups who are perceived as profiting from or collaborating in the *status quo* are not usually objects of sympathy. For example, supposing one took the point of view that sex roles as presently constituted operate in favour of men, and that it is they who have most to lose by reorganization. It is conceivable that such a position could help generate or sustain negative social stereotypes of males. Correspondingly, it could be argued that females who adopt styles of physical appearance consistent with the standards rep-resented as desirable in the mass media are not only allowing themselves to be duped and exploited but are helping also to perpetu-ate a social system that devalues other qualities in women and downgrades those who eschew conventional attractiveness. It is conceivable that such an analysis could lead to negative evaluations of some women. These lines of reasoning may hold some interest in certain polemical contexts, but what are their implications for in-terventions in TV? Would it be desirable to propagate destructive messages about the traditional male role and about glamorous women? Given the rigidity of the male sex role, it could be quite threatening to some boys to be confronted with repeated attacks on their nascent self-images or personal goals (we have already seen evidence that they will sometimes resist counterstereotypes that

appear to undermine traditional male characteristics). Given the
sensitivity of issues of feminine appearance in most cultures, it could
be very distressing to some girls to encounter derision of prettiness. It
would be a shallow defence to maintain that inflicting a different set of
values upon children would help to redress the balance and to resolve
inequities suffered by older generations.

Problem 6: Artistic considerations

Problems 4 and 5 are closely allied to artistic concerns facing broadcasters. It could be argued, for example, that writers cannot be
expected to produce creative work to meet the dictates of a particular
ideology. Certainly, one would suppose that a list of *dos* and *don'ts*
affixed to the broadcaster's wall by a well-meaning pressure group
might not provide the optimal conditions for original productions and
could lead to reworking of 'safe' lines that eventually become tiresome
to the audience. There is also a problem that faithful treatments of
many social contexts and many historical eras would necessarily
incur representation of sex role inequalities. It would be overdoing
artistic licence to depict Henry VIII as an early feminist, and the
scope for documentaries on female Presidents of the United States
is limited. Dramatizations of much classic literature would be
prohibited from our screens if sexual equality were a criterion of
acceptability.

Problem 7: Image and reality

Even if the broadcasters could cope effectively with these artistic/
factual constraints there is a further and ironic problem that their
success in doing so could lead to the perpetuation of a new type of sex
role mythology in TV: the message that all is well. If there were equal
numbers of males and females on our screens occupying identical
statuses and betraying no traditional trait stereotypes, would this
detract from public awareness of *actual* discrepancies and deceive
young viewers in particular into the belief that equal opportunities
exist in all spheres of human activity?

The case for the defence

There are some bases for a defence of counterstereotyping and some
safeguards, though inevitably these can only be supported by the
assumption of ideologies antithetical to the *status quo* and mitigated by
concern for sensitivity at the level of implementation.

'Interference in the course of development' may be justifiable, for example, if we regard aspects of traditional sex role development as potentially dysfunctional and restrictive of the individual. Offering children information concerning additional personal prospects can be a positive contribution. Only the most reactionary opponent of social change would find it reprehensible to allow girls to see females in TV with diverse occupational roles; since females do have diverse occupational roles even in contemporary society, it constitutes deception to ignore or neglect the fact in our media, and honesty to represent it. As was stressed in Chapter 2, the sex role stereotypes in TV distort reality and under-represent the variety and scope of *actual* human behaviour. TV could be used to demonstrate to children that, say, all men need not perpetually affirm the problem-solving skills of *The A-Team* or *The Incredible Hulk* but can additionally or alternatively exercise the properties of warmth, nurturance and humour. Again such themes can be identified with male performances in TV without any need for fabrication or any risk of confronting children with disturbances to their sex role knowledge based on real-life experience. Increasing the diversity of role representations on TV need constitute an 'interference' only to the extent that it increases the congruence between the medium and certain aspects of the reality the child encounters elsewhere. Illustrating the possibility that a man might become a nurse, for instance, is not a crime against nature but an acknowledgement of an everyday fact.

Lack of unanimity about sex role allocation does not of course mean that dissent or novel ideas should never be voiced. It is also the case that, in any society, responsibility for raising successive generations is at least in part a collective obligation constrained by the institutions, by formal and informal regulations, by the educational system and other public standards, as well as by the direct actions of parents towards their own children. In practice, the problem of any one pressure group reshaping the entirety of TV content to meet its blueprint for a better society is unlikely to occur, and it is impossible for reshaped TV content to revolutionize the world outside irrespective of the desires and activities of others. It also remains the case that parents who wish to prevent their children from broadening their views of male and female roles will have the options of switching off or commenting adversely upon non-traditional content.

Defining a coherent goal for sex role change is certainly one of the most challenging prospects for work with counterstereotypes, though of course this is scarcely a problem unique to TV researchers or broadcasters. Although 'sex roles' is a topic of widespread contemporary interest, the lack of a cogent theory of change means that many attempts at counterstereotyping will inevitably be piecemeal and focused on arbitrary aspects of behaviour or status. This is not entirely unhealthy if it promotes more deliberated attempts to define the goals of change, and in this way practice and theory may interact fruitfully.

In much the same way reaction, even negative reaction, to some counterstereotyped material in TV may make long-term positive contributions. The outcome of an intervention may not always be immediate nor direct. A careers idea rejected by a 12-year-old as preposterous may be resurrected and reconsidered by the same child at 15 years when vocational choice becomes a more authentic concern; a social theme belittled by a nine-year-old on first exposure may be accommodated after direct cognitive attention; the condemnation of a TV message by a parent may make it all the more intriguing to an adolescent, and so on. Reaction increases the likelihood of discussion, and discussion increases the likelihood of reflection. There are certainly liabilities attached to Messianic approaches to counterstereotyping, but these do not preclude the possibility of progress by more sensitive modes of broadcasting.

Negative dimensions of counterstereotyping can be avoided by choice and by care, and both are clearly called for in such work. Successful projects in this respect have generally been based upon constructive rather than destructive premises, as articulated clearly by Williams *et al*.:

> Rather than eradicating the individual's entire self-concept and replacing it with another representing the opposite pole of a continuum, the task becomes one of supplementing personality attributes with characteristics that result in a psychologically healthier individual. (Williams *et al*. 1981:9)

A 'psychologically healthier individual' remains a difficult concept to define but a working hypothesis might be that deprivation of opportunity and personal expression are obstructions to it. Promoting greater personal autonomy and freedom of choice irrespective of gender do seem reasonable candidates for acceptable intervention goals.

Artistic problems are not as thoroughgoing as they might appear. The question of whether writers could work creatively while upholding counterstereotype goals begs the question of how so many writers have managed hitherto to work creatively while upholding traditional themes. It also suggests the self-contradictory proposition that creative writers should find it difficult to tackle novel ideas. Writers generally have to obey laws and regulations controlling the expression of racism and obscenity, and while there are of course issues of censorship that relate to any constraints upon broadcasters, it is clearly the case that many creative writers can work adequately with some regard to social responsibility. Although it is true that much of history and culture is a record of sexual inequality, it is not invariably the case that all treatments need endorse traditions which are now outmoded, nor is it inevitable that all entertainment must be restricted to sex role stereotypes: Henry VIII's gender and proclivities are irreversible, but the courting behaviours of the *Dukes of Hazzard* are modifiable, and the captainship of the *Starship Enterprise* is transferable. More generally, much of the material in daily TV is not primarily 'creative', at least in the sense used above (e.g. news broadcasts, advertisements) and in these areas it is likely that non-sexist practices could be fostered without artistic damage being feared (see Butler and Paisley (1980:333ff.) for a good account of the practicalities). Finally on this point, the proof of the pudding is in the eating, and the major realization of counterstereotyping in professional broadcasting, *Freestyle*, is reported to have attracted and sustained healthy viewing figures during its availability in several states in North America (Johnston and Ettema 1982).

The prospect of a non-sexist, non-stereotyped mass medium deluding young (or other) viewers into assuming the world was a more egalitarian place than it is, is an interesting conjecture but an unrealistic prospect. In an inequitable society, there is little reason to fear that TV will fail to over-represent the interests of the dominant groups, and whether it is in entertainment or non-fiction contexts there is every reason to suppose that traditional sex role stereotypes will remain the norm for some time. Even if far-reaching modifications of TV content were attained through continuous pressure, however, it would be a gross exaggeration of the potency of the medium to assume that this would outweigh or preempt children's appraisals of the real-world (see for example the studies on career beliefs by O'Bryant and Corder-Bolz (1978) and Durkin and Hutchins (1984) discussed earlier). To abandon counterstereotyping on the grounds that it may generate pictures which are too rosy, is a defeatist and non-productive strategy which overestimates the consequences of the intervention and underestimates the independence of the viewer.

Several of the possible problems above relate to a quite hypothetical conception of counterstereotyping as an instantaneous transformation of the entire TV system. In fact, of course, counterstereotyping is a minority concern and will only be furthered as an influence upon the medium as a result of continuous pressure from within and without. The overriding ethical issue in this context is whether to accept things as they are or to contribute to the processes of change. Societies are progressing, however awkwardly, towards redefined and less restrictive sex roles and these developments are not exclusively or primarily in the hands of broadcasters or researchers.

Their work, however, can act as a catalyst and a complement to broader social movements, and for that reason it is important that it be conducted with awareness of the possible negative outcomes of

insensitive interventions and with careful attention to the evaluation
of new ideas and practices. It is this point of possible contact with the
world outside of the laboratory that makes it all the more important
that the relevant research be conducted extensively and rigorously.
Children are not battlegrounds or fodder for the trial of fashionable
conjectures, and it is not enough to imagine that it would be a 'good
idea' to set about reshaping them. Research can sometimes appear
too tiresome, too time-consuming and often too qualified in its results
to be of direct use to those who wish to redesign the world; the dangers
of abandoning it include the risk of coming up with another inadequate design and another poor account of the needs of the inhabi-
tants. If there is one concrete conclusion emerging from the recent
research on counterstereotyping, it is that children will not be
reshaped but may rethink – and it is ultimately they who will
determine what their needs will be as they define their futures.

SEVEN

Television, sex roles and children: towards a developmental social psychological theory

> Either there are indeed no effects, or measurement is inadequate or impossible, or some more realistic version of what is going on is called for. (McQuail 1976:352)

The preceding chapters considered most of the evidence currently available bearing upon the place of television in sex role development. No account of a growing research area can guarantee exhaustiveness, and no doubt I have failed to take note of a small number of relevant studies, but it is probably fair to claim that the bulk of contemporary research that has been published on this topic has been summarized here. It is now time to reflect on the state of the art. In this chapter, I will attempt to draw together the various themes and arguments that have been developed through this survey and to construct an overview of what we know and of what we need to know about TV and sex role acquisition.

Three points stand out from the work to date. First, an overriding conclusion must be that there are many gaps in our understanding of how television contributes to this area of social development. What we need to know exceeds what we do know, and for that reason much of this chapter will be concerned with indicating issues for future research. Secondly, the evidence for the most popular intuitive theory, i.e. that the more TV a child watches, the more traditional his or her sex role development will become, is not overwhelming. It remains a possibility that some appropriate research design(s) could eventually provide more convincing evidence but we have to recognize that belief in linear causality is at present a matter of faith rather than scientifically supported judgement. Thirdly, there is *some* evidence that *some* television-based interventions, designed to modify traditional sex role beliefs in the young, can have *some* effect in the intended directions.

These assertions echo the kinds of highly qualified conclusions that have been made in many other investigations of television 'effects', and they may sound disappointingly imprecise to readers who seek clear-cut evidence one way or the other. Worse still, they may strike some readers as disturbingly suggestive of the proposition that we can afford to reduce any anxieties about sex stereotyping in the medium.

My own conclusion is that the available evidence makes the topic of TV and sex role acquisition a still more serious focus of theory and research than has been the case so far. The abundant content analyses (Chapter 1) revealing that the primary mass medium commonly distorts its representations of the sexes, so that males are frequently shown in rigidly prescribed roles and females are depicted as largely subordinate or peripheral to humanity's concerns, is certainly sufficient indication that much is amiss in what mass communications researchers call 'the sender'. The fact that such representations are taken as acceptable, perhaps even desirable, by the central arbiters of mass culture whose standards determine the regularities of the content of everyday viewing experience for vast populations, is scarcely a trivial issue.

It is precisely because the topic is so important to an understanding of a fundamental aspect of our social order that we need to review the evidence carefully and question the assumption of direct, linear causality that I suggest has been too readily adopted by many critics of TV sexism.

This is not to accept the null hypothesis that TV has *no* effects on sex role development but rather to assert that superficial accounts will promote superficial understanding, and hence superficial solutions. A serious analysis of a far-reaching social psychological issue such as the interaction between medium and young viewer needs to acknowledge the complexity of both and needs to take into account the changing capacities of the child as a developing person in a multifaceted social context. I have suggested at various points in the book that this task is best undertaken within the framework of a developmental social psychology, and in this concluding chapter I will attempt to draw together the basis for such a perspective and to indicate the kinds of issues that it poses for future research.

Summarizing briefly themes that have been elaborated in earlier chapters, it has been argued (Chapter 4) that TV viewing time is an adequate independent variable on which to predict degree of traditional sex stereotyping in children. The linear effects hypothesis overlooks too much of the complexity of the data it purports to account for, not least the developmental changes in children, the diversity of children's social and domestic contexts, and the scope for plurality even in predominantly stereotyped media such as TV. The same obstacles confront any crude stimulus-response theory of viewer –medium relations. However, it has also been argued (Chapter 5) that children do strive to make sense of TV social information and that the ways in which they do so are functions of the social-cognitive schema and strategies that they construct in the course of developing as social beings. Hence, like other commentators on TV 'effects' upon children, I have argued that the question is not so much what television does *to* as what children do *with* television (cf. Comstock *et al.* 1978:175). And, in a nutshell, what they have to do with sex roles as commonly portrayed in television is *to process distorted information* (i.e. information which is highly sex stereotyped) during periods of their lives when their sex role knowledge is still developing. The real questions for research on this topic are: how do children accommodate this distorted information in their social reasoning and social adjustment?

Many issues are at stake in attempting to unravel this complex and multi-determined transaction, but it will help to reflect on these if we distinguish *the developmental context, the family context* and the *socio-cultural context*, all as important (and interactive) constraints upon how children come to use social information in TV. The following sections consider each of these in turn.

The developmental context

Of the various participants in the medium–audience relationship, children are the most complex group of 'receivers', and one of the most difficult to study. Part of the problem facing any serious enquiry in this area is that children are constantly growing and changing. This means that the social and intellectual properties that they bring to their viewing, and the range of personal, emotional and informational needs that they seek to gratify by watching television are vast. Unfortunately, this means in turn that any simple statement that TV is responsible for *X* amount of sex role stereotyping in children beliefs or behaviour is unwarranted, and unhelpful.

It is more productive to strive towards a comprehensive account of how developing people attend to, comprehend and use the information in TV, and it will be useful to recapitulate the evidence available on these processes with reference to what many developmentalists take as key, if broadly defined, stages of development. The following skeleton account therefore summarizes points made in more detail in earlier chapters concerning developments in the *use* of television sex role information during the preschool, early school, middle childhood and adolescent periods.

The preschool years (0 to approximately 4 years)

During these years, children begin to discriminate among people using gender as one basis for classification, they discover their own gender category, and they begin to acquire knowledge of the associations and consequences of gender membership. Much of this activity *precedes* systematic interest in television, and much of it is occurring *simultaneously* when, usually during their third year of life, children do begin to take increasing interest in TV as an aspect of their environment. Some evidence (see Chapter 5) indicates that at this early stage of television viewing they discriminate among the people available with some bias towards an interest in females. Exactly why this is so, and what children derive from the selective attention manifest in this way – and how this might relate to subsequent development in intrapersonal organization and viewing patterns – are questions for future research. The significance of such evidence at present is that it seems to reflect some gender-related discrimination on the part of quite young viewers. It scarcely needs to be added that it also coincides with traditional (female-organized) domestic arrangements to which many children are exposed, and we turn to the family context shortly. Overall, it seems unlikely that television is a primary source of sex role information during this period, because the child has more meaningful interactions with its caregivers, siblings and peers, and because at this stage of social-cognitive development much of the content of daily television will be too complex for the child to understand at any depth.

The early school years (approximately 4–7 years)

During these years, children are building their understanding of the regularities and long-term consequences of gender membership (gender constancy). Their own gender categories are well established and for each individual forms an important part of his or her self-identity, though they have much to learn about the subtleties of sex role regulation, and their sex role knowledge and beliefs often appear to be based on rigid and oversimplified generalizations of external differences (Kohlberg 1966; Ullian 1976). During this period children appear to bias their *attention*, under experimental conditions at least, towards same-sex figures on screen. Again, we know rather little of what children extract from this strategy, and of individual differences in this respect, but two possible motives stand out. One is that they are monitoring the people on screen for new data on gender-appropriate behaviour and dress; another is that they are attempting to confirm their existing hypotheses about these personal attributes. These are not mutually exclusive proposals, though they differ to some extent in the locus of initiative: in the first case, the power of the medium to provide and provoke is emphasized, whereas the second points to the receivers' abilities to formulate and evaluate their own theories. It seems plausible that both (inductive and deductive) processes occur, and the relative strength of sender–receiver motivation at different times may vary as a function of other developments in the child. However, we saw in Chapter 5 that there is evidence from several sources to indicate that young viewers are capable both of exploiting their own social theories and of dissecting patterns in the form of the medium. Thus, television may well be used by the child at this stage as one source of information about sex roles.

Nevertheless, it is well known that children below around age seven or so show surprising gaps when tested for their understanding and recall of programmes that they have just watched, apparently intently (see Collins 1983). This should warn us against assuming that the child is calculating the parameters of contemporary sex role regulations with the same eye for detail and the same sensitivity to the structure of the interpersonal relationships as a content analyst. It should also be borne in mind that the child at this stage not only retains the option of gathering sex role information through participating in a much more directly meaningful domestic context, but also is increasing her or his experience of other people in other environments, often with clear demarcations around sex, such as the school and the peer group.

Middle childhood (approximately 7–12 years)

During these years, children elaborate and refine their sex role knowledge and become more aware of the psychological properties of people, including those stereotypically associated with each sex. They also develop and consolidate their abilities to follow, grasp and retain the story structure of TV programmes (Collins 1983). The attentional preferences of children in this age group with respect to sex role behaviours in television have not been extensively studied, though there is evidence (Chapter 5) that they develop preferences for particular characters, that they can perceive differences in the psychological properties of male and female characters, and during this period programme preferences diverge according to sex of viewer (Comstock *et al.* 1978: Ch. 5). This suggests again that TV use is directed by the general developmental status of the child, though we know relatively little about how they evaluate specific information about sex roles that they encounter in their viewing.

It is known though, that during these years children develop increasingly sophisticated understanding of the nature of the medium in general (cf. Dorr 1980). During middle childhood, children discard their earlier assumptions that TV depicts 'reality', and become aware that most of the people on screen are actors and that much of their behaviour is simulated rather than authentic. They become more discerning viewers (even if their tastes may not always impress or please their caregivers) and more able to detect the improbable and the fantastic in TV. The extent to which these nascent critical powers are ever addressed to such matters as portrayals of male and female roles has not been extensively studied. However, the evidence on children's general understanding of TV during these years serves to indicate that they do not necessarily 'take in' and accept as realistic or desirable everything that they watch. We noted, in Chapter 4, that at least one study (Cheles-Miller 1975) found that high-viewing children were *more sceptical* in a *Stereotype Acceptance Test*. Again, it is worth stressing that there are likely to be individual differences in critical ability, sensitivity and disposition. Certainly, there is evidence of this with respect to children's reactions to *counter*stereotyped materials; both List *et al.* (1983) and Eisenstock (1984) have found that differences in the sex role beliefs and orientation of children in middle childhood influence how successfully children attend to or recall elements of non-traditional behaviour in television characters.

Adolescence (approximately 12–18 years)

The social-cognitive and related personal developments that proceed through these years are obviously so substantial that it is something of an oversimplification to summarize this in developmental terms as one continuous period. The main justification for doing so in the present context is simply that adolescents' reactions to sex role information in television have been the least studied of all the developmental phases, and any discussion must be largely speculative.

Even so, it is reasonable to assume that throughout adolescence sex role and sexuality are high priority concerns for most people. During this period, the biological developments begun with puberty are associated with major personal adjustment and changes in self-image. Social life becomes increasingly oriented around gender, in terms of both friendship and courtship, and physical appearance of self and others becomes highly salient.

Adolescence may also occasion discontinuity in sex role development, and this may be experienced differently by members of each sex. In an important theoretical paper, Archer (1984) has argued that males and females follow different 'pathways' in the course of sex role socialization. The male role typically becomes increasingly rigid (with strong pressures to avoid opposite sex behaviours) from the preschool to adolescent years, as a number of extrinsic and intrinsic processes establish the basis for the greater opportunities and responsibilities for males post-adolescence. The female role in childhood is typically more flexible (with less pressure to avoid opposite-sex behaviours) but is more drastically curtailed at adolescence when a heightened interest in femininity and restrictive domestic and vocational expectations are encouraged from many quarters.

Adolescence is a critical period in the lifespan, because here decisions are made (purposefully or by default) which are likely to have a lasting influence on the individual's long-term future (Huston-Stein and Higgins-Trenk 1977; Katz 1979). The consequences of regular exposure to glamorous sex-stereotyped TV figures during this period may be substantial, though they may differ for each sex because of the different places they have reached in their 'pathways'. On the one hand, TV sex role images may complement the narrowing world-view that many girls will develop during adolescence. Television will undoubtedly present many images of idealized feminine desirability, considerable emphasis on youthfulness, and numerous 'happy ever after' scripts of marital bliss in scenarios which afford little scope for female employment. The limited evidence we have on the effects of intense exposure to this kind of emphasis (Tan 1979;

see Chapter 5) does indicate that the TV message can highlight particular traditional expectations that many girls will have developed at this stage.

For boys, adolescence may incur a different kind of discontinuity in that, even in sex-typed male-dominated cultures, the male sex role stereotype is not totally congruous with the actual demands of adult male life. As Pleck (1976) argues, there is an important distinction between the *traditional* male role, involving an emphasis upon achievement and the suppression of affect, and the *modern* male role, which is probably less easily identified and less uniform, but which involves stress on intellectual and interpersonal skills rather than physical toughness, and which calls for companionship with women rather than domination. Boys who have developed rigid and rather traditional expectations during earlier stages of development may enter adolescence with simplified and incomplete sex role understanding. The greater availability of stereotyped male figures in TV may provide generous opportunities to confirm or embellish unrealistic role concepts which leave them ill-prepared for the realities of impending adulthood, and thus contribute to a period of role conflict which may extend well beyond adolescence (see Pleck 1976).

Much more work is needed to help understand how girls and boys in this formative period evaluate the sex role images in TV. *Prima facie* evidence suggests, not that TV has unimpeded control over either sex, but that it may be integrated into patterns and problems of social development in complex and important ways. Although it is popular to assume that TV is helping to 'mould' children during this stage (and others), such a notion may lead us to overlook other possible effects, such as the instigation of personal insecurity due to social comparisons that some children may make between their self-concepts and unrealistically glamorous and powerful television figures. This remains to be tested.

To summarize, the developmental context – that is, the developing social-cognitive attainments of active and inquisitive young persons – is critical to the acquisition of sex role information from television. Although many of the details elude us, it is clear that children progress qualitatively in their understanding of social phenomena, and that there are individual differences in the salience accorded to different aspects of sex roles at different points in the early lifespan. Thus, to talk of 'the child' being affected by television distortions suggests an homogeneous transaction for which there is little theoretical justification and few supporting data.

Furthermore, it should be stressed that since developmental changes are by definition modifications of previous states of knowledge and behaviour then their consequences are likely at the very least to adjust, and possibly sometimes to negate, environmental 'effects' from an earlier period. Simply put, if one preschool child infers from TV action dramas that his future role will include perpetual combat with Brontosauri, or another appraises commercials as revealing that her later duties will be oriented around the energetic application of kitchen cleansing products, it does not necessarily follow that these children will sustain these expectations, even at some more general- ized level, through to adolescence. Nor can we assume that they have the same meaning and value to children that they do for adults. Indeed, recent research into children's social cognitions about mat- ters such as sex roles suggests that young people undergo several changes in their beliefs and attitudes towards sex role constraints, successively accepting and rejecting the perceived rules of society for increasingly sophisticated reasons as they refine their conceptual organization of the world around them (see Turiel 1983). Quite obviously, to examine the consequences of viewing television stereotypes with full account of the developmental and individual differences at stake remains a massive research task.

The family context

It is important to bear in mind the obvious but far-reaching con- sideration that children are not simply *observers* of social life but *participants*, and much of their social experience is located in family contexts. In a general discussion of the effects of television upon children, Howitt (1976:325) points out that it is implausible to assume that parents patiently await the onset of media literacy before initiating or guiding discovery of social knowledge in their offspring. For most young children, the family is the principal location for early social interaction and exploration, and it provides the most accessible and most potent source of information and feedback about what is desirable and undesirable in personal behaviour.

There are very strong reasons for taking family interaction as the primary base for sex role acquisition. First of all, gender of infant is one of the foremost concerns of most parents (see Chapter 3), and assignment to gender membership is one of the first classifications made of the new child. Once this is known, a host of expectations and perceptions are brought to bear upon the new person (see Chapter 3 for more discussion). It was suggested in Chapter 3 that this provides the child with countless daily opportunities to participate in social interchanges which generate information and regulations bearing on sex role development. Remember too that the family is best placed to respond to changes in the child with age, and to provide direct information about new social expectations at different stages of

development. Since sex roles are so fundamental to personal development, it is quite obviously the case that few families will unwittingly
leave to TV this aspect of socialization. In this domain as much as any
other, it is sensible to agree with what Howitt advances as a 'general
principle' that 'for virtually all areas of social development, real-life
influences will have operated over and above those of the mass media'
(1976:325).

We saw in Chapter 4 that some studies have found associations
between children's sex role beliefs and the occupational status of their
mothers: the daily activities of one highly significant and real-life
other may, in certain domains, be a more persuasive source of
information than countless TV fictions. Similarly, Repetti (1984)
found no relationship between amount of TV viewing and traditional
sex role development, but did find moderately strong correlations
between parental personality characteristics and the sex stereotypes
held by their children. It would not really be very surprising if we were
to find that children discover more about sex role divisions from the
principal characters in their real world than in their media, and
indeed one of the earliest major studies of the impact of TV upon the
young concluded that its effect on children's view of marriage and
family life was negligible, partly because children 'get their views
about family life chiefly from home' (Himmelweit *et al.* 1958:248).
Greenberg and Reeves (1976) have also found that children in middle
childhood rate TV portrayals of family life as less realistic than
portrayals of the police and of black people. Once again, the most
reasonable interpretation of the available evidence seems to be that
children appraise aspects of TV content in terms of their existing
social understanding, which itself will be constructed exploiting data
from many sources, and that they will variously accept, ignore and
occasionally reject components of what they view.

It would be an oversimplification, however, to regard TV merely
as an *additional* variable possibly impinging to some limited degree
upon the developing person. Rather, it is likely that TV is an
interacting variable, integrated almost literally into the family. TV
viewing by children occurs primarily in social contexts, usually family
contexts (Chaffee 1972; Chaffee and Tims 1976), and this raises at
least two important considerations for our understanding of the ways
in which TV information is received.

Consider first the fact that TV viewing is itself commonly something of a family routine, embedded in interpersonal practices that
reflect the arrangement of social status and roles within that family.
Although popular mythology has it that this amounts to little more
than a 'group slump' of inert figures, oblivious to anything but the
screen, even this minimal box-dominated set up may provide real-life
information and illustration of sex role patterns. For example, where

does Dad sit? Seating arrangements in some homes reflect age–sex status. Who makes the final decision in cases of conflict over programme selection? Which members of the family are dispatched to make the tea during the commercial breaks? Who decrees when it is the children's bedtime, and how are the arrangements for their toiletries shared out? Television may be part of the family, but it does not run it. Instead, it is used as part of a structured living context. Gans (1980) remarks that in families he studied in the course of a television project, the set was almost always used as a background company while the rest of the household activities proceeded, including entertaining visitors.

Clearly, family viewing patterns are interrelated with many other aspects of the family regime. Substantial evidence to this effect comes from a large study by Singer and Singer (1981), which found that certain types of high-viewing families were characterized additionally by general laxity in control of the set, a lack of outside family interests, more traditional male and female roles in the parents, as well as preferences for particular types of action/sports programmes over 'family' or comedy shows (see esp. p. 122ff.). Thus, measuring 'high viewing' in a child from such a family (the strategy adopted by some studies discussed in Chapter 4) is confounded with other pervasive and powerful factors in the child's domestic setting.

The second important consideration relating to the family context of TV viewing is that the television content may be the focus of comment and discussion which may mediate, reduce or exacerbate 'messages' implicit in the programmes (Chaffee and Tims 1976; Messaris and Sarett 1981; McLeod *et al.* 1982). Although we have little evidence on how often such spontaneous commentaries touch upon sex role issues, ethnographic accounts suggest that some viewers can be quite emphatic about what is 'masculine' and what is 'feminine' in television (see Hobson 1980). Programme choice itself may communicate to youngsters something about the gender appropriateness of particular types of material. For example, on average women view soap operas much more than men do, while men form much greater proportions of the audience for sports programmes (cf. Comstock *et al.* 1978:113). Doubtless many children are provided with blatant or subtle encouragement to watch (or not watch) TV content stereotypically associated with a particular sex.

There are many respects, of course, in which TV provides information concerning human relationships and behaviour that is not always available for direct observation in the child's own domestic context. These may include violations of sex role constraints, for example, as discussed in Chapter 6, as well as fiction and news items about life-styles and events beyond the ordinary. We return to some of these issues shortly. One other aspect of TV content related to sex role acquisition which is relevant here is the portrayal of human sexuality. According to one survey (summarized in Roberts 1982) many parents believe that children learn more about sexuality from television than from parents or peers. Whether the parents' estimate of the relative contributions of these and other sources is exactly correct is not well established, but it is worth noting that TV does present information about sexuality and sexual relations which make for more detached and often more detailed observation than is likely to be opportune in many actual real-life settings. It is conceivable that TV information about these matters may be more vivid than some other sources, such as reluctant or cryptic allusions by parents with anxieties about sex.

However, it is difficult to ascertain what children, especially adolescents, infer from televised sexuality. The courtship patterns scripted in television are often so idealized that it would be naive to assume that all teenagers, who are capable of sceptical viewing (Dorr 1980), believe everything they watch, and the presentation of eroticism is normally so curtailed that anyone completely dependent upon television for the facts of life would have to infer that the climax of sexual activity is a scene switch or failure of the lighting system. There are interesting questions for future research concerning the match between TV sexual scripts and young people's romantic expectations (see Roberts (1982) for a useful discussion). Although once again common sense dictates that real-life experience ultimately overrides TV fiction, the extent to which unrealistically idyllic themes form a backdrop to adolescent viewers' sexual thinking and behaviour merits investigation.

To summarize the family context, it is obviously the case that this is the primary location for much of early social development. This does not necessarily mean that children will grow up to emulate the sex role standards of their parents, nor that parents can choose to control the sex role aspirations of their children. It does mean that children learn a great deal from interacting with the other key people in their immediate lives, especially family members, and that it is in this context that they make their earliest discoveries about social roles and opportunities. Television is integrated into these structures and processes. Because TV is rife with traditional sex role stereotypes and implicit and explicit sexist messages, much of its fare will be to some degree consistent with the sex role arrangements of those households which are not consciously committed to alternatives to the *status quo*. Thus, it seems very likely that although TV is difficult to identify as a primary 'cause' of sex role divisions it will often serve, as Greenberg (1982:188) suggests, to 'supplement, reinforce, and complement' the social processes into which it is incorporated. It is difficult, perhaps impossible, to measure how much it contributes in this way, and it is very likely that these processes would (and do) occur in the absence of

TV sets, but what remains disturbing about contemporary broadcasting is that it presents limited perspectives in generous amounts.

The socio-cultural context

It is beyond the scope of this book to attempt to account in detail for the socio-cultural context in which incoming members of society acquire and enact their sex roles. The general assumption that has been adopted here is that the socio-historical basis for sex role constraints lies in the arrangement of human beings in relation to the economic order. The genesis of large and complex societies had led to divisions of occupational and domestic labour that reflect an interaction between the demands of the organized pursuit of available resources and the exploitation of differing capacities of individual people.

For large periods of recent history, it has been congenial to the prevailing arrangements for the distribution of wealth to maintain workforces of males offering manual labour or specific, trained skills, supplemented in some industries by large numbers of (frequently temporary) female employees employed in routine and menial tasks for which little investment or training is required. The primary duties of females during their reproductive years have been assumed in many societies to be those of child-rearing.

Although some of these factors are currently being undermined by a combination of the demands of changing technologies, by the rise of mass unemployment, and by ideological challenges, much of the structural organization of our societies continues to reflect the needs of orders based on sex role discrimination. Thus, to state the obvious, many of the opportunities and institutions that an individual encounters in the early lifespan promote different possibilities for the different sexes. The family, the school, the peer group, leisure provision in the community, work/unemployment environments, sex discriminatory laws and political institutions are all sources of rich information and feedback throughout life about what is deemed appropriate to each sex, and for present purposes it is sufficient simply to echo a point from the previous section, that real-life is likely to be a more powerful determinant of individual development than is vicarious experience in the media.

However, it is important to our discussion of the place of TV in sex role development to recognize that, as stressed when we considered the family context, the medium is not additional to but is *integrated* into the broader structures of social life. It is scarcely a coincidence that much of the sex stereotyping in TV is consistent with traditional biases in the mainstream of the societies that produce TV. However, our concern here is less with how the 'sender' comes to adopt the characteristics we have defined, and more with how the 'receiver' accommodates to these properties.

The socio-cultural context and the individual

One of the most difficult overarching tasks facing social psychology is to account for the relationship between the structures of society and the behaviour, beliefs and understanding of the individuals that compose it. The mass media provide interesting focal points in this enquiry, because they both *reflect* elements of the society and are *used* by members of that society. Thus, study of the media–user interrelationship contributes towards the greater task of understanding the society–person interrelationship.

To advance this goal, a theoretical framework is needed which can at once incorporate an account of regularities in societies' symbolic products and indicate something of the strategies that are employed by individual decoders of those products. I have suggested at various points in the text that recent work on the social psychology of *scripts* has considerable value to researchers at the intersection of mass media and psychological processes, and it may be useful now to summarize how such a theoretical perspective can help to bring together usefully issues and lines of enquiry that are often pursued independently.

Although theoretical models in this area remain sketchy, and empirical substantiation is still at an early stage, we have seen that a script approach has the potential to capture clearly important phenomena in describing the *content* of TV with respect to sex roles. Scripts form part of a given society's culture (Abelson 1976; Nelson 1981). They are shared expectations about what will happen in certain contexts, and about what is desirable and undesirable in terms of outcome.

Male and female roles and relationships are so fundamental to much of our social organization that many elements and events re-occur innumerable times in everyday life. Many of these are represented, again innumerable times, in the scripts of our mass media. For example, as we noted at the beginning of the book, heterosexual romance is a major theme of much entertainment fiction, and writers and audience seem to have a high tolerance level for frequent reworking of a limited number of event sequences around this topic. Analysing these and related male–female scripts, such as domestic and occupational behaviours, as recurring event sequences, offers a possibly more far-reaching account not only of medium content but also of its relation to the surrounding society than do lists of behavioural characteristics scored discretely, as in a content analysis.

At the same time, such an approach also allows us to ask what the receiver *does* with the TV script. Janis (1980:165) has suggested that much of the potential power of TV to influence people may reside 'in its capacity to increase the availability of images of specific outcomes' via repetitive exploitation of particular scripts. Along similar lines, Geis *et al.* (1984) have argued that recurring images of sex-stereotyped females in TV commercials may help create and sustain personal scripts for low occupational achievement aspirations in women. A major question for future research in this field is in what ways the scripts of TV influence and interact with the scripts of viewers.

From the developmental point of view, the relationship between TV scripts and children's social understanding is an intriguing question to which we have limited, but provocative, answers at present. On the one hand, recent research has begun to show that children's decoding of the event sequences of TV programmes is not akin to adults' and that this aspect of media literacy is developed over a considerable period of early and middle childhood (Collins 1983). On the other hand, we know that children are engaged in and developing 'scripts' for social interaction routines in their everyday lives from very early on (Nelson 1981; Nelson and Gruendel 1982) and that they develop some scripts concerning male–female inter-relations by the preschool years which they are able to use to make sense of sex role information in television (Durkin 1984; see Chapter 5).

It seems likely that those TV scripts which deal with conventional and routine aspects of social life, concerning which the child also has independent real-world evidence, are more easy to interpret and the evidence so far indicates that TV scripts are interpreted with reference to children's existing scripts. This makes it very difficult to attribute measurable causation to one source or another, but it does steer us towards more integrated and more dynamic accounts of the place of TV in the development of social knowledge. Sex roles are important to the individual and to the society: they are invested with affect by both sides of this equation because they relate directly to social identity (one's place in the social structure) and to sexuality (and hence ultimately to one's place in the reproduction of self and society). Consequently, for any child sex role knowledge is critical to maintaining social-cognitive consistency in a complex environment, and social stereotypes about sex roles in turn facilitate the process of finding her or his 'way in' to the broader structure of the community by simplifying issues of relative status. In so far as the child's and the TV's scripts in this domain are congruent, each unexceptional enactment of a conventional sex role script will be interpretable by the young viewer and thus add to the numerous observational and practical opportunities that she or he will have to learn about this particular aspect of behaviour.

The opportunities may be additive, but the learning is organized, and I have argued that it is not the *amount* of the former that predicts how the child uses the information but the quality and structure of the social understanding that the child has. Thus, if we are ever to discover the 'effects' of viewing particular aspects of TV sexism, we need to start from where the child is in his or her development and in his or her social world. For the sake of clarity I repeat my general argument: in certain specifiable but scarcely tested circumstances, we might expect some detectable adverse effects, but in the main TV is likely to confirm rather than to initiate beliefs about the sex role constraints that the child is discovering in the broader society. This is not a trivial contribution and does not mean that TV should be thought unimportant: if one, virtually omnipresent, manifestation of the broader culture does serve to endorse and embellish the *status quo* then its function may be powerful and well-deserving of continuing scrutiny. The point is that it may be counterproductive to depict TV as a distinct source responsible for 'causing' a certain amount of sex role beliefs or behaviour in the young when its actual relationship to society may be more subtle and more complex.

Because the socio-cultural context is always in a state of flux and because there are always elements of change developing within it, there are occasions when it can act upon the mass media, and hence upon the viewer, in ways which reflect its own self-contradictions. When in response to such pressures or experimentation the TV script is exceptional, for example when it departs from or flouts stereotyped conventions and introduces non-traditional event sequences, then it poses a challenge to the child's existing repertoire which he or she may meet in various ways. If the TV script is too advanced for his or her social-cognitive level, then the message may not even be perceived; in these circumstances, the child may actually interpret the screen events in accord with existing expectations, as found by Drabman and colleagues in one experiment (see Chapter 6). At a later stage, the child may detect the unconventional but be unable to incorporate the idea as an enduring representation (as Drabman found with some older subjects), or may be so committed, cognitively and affectively, to an existing apperception of the *status quo* that he or she may reject the counterstereotype as absurd or undesirable (as some intervention experiments have reported; Chapter 6). Finally, the child may detect and accept the non-traditional message, as several interventions have found in different circumstances, though it is worth recalling that the evidence from the largest counterstereotyping project, *Freestyle*, indicates that this is most likely and most effective when the medium message is supported by additional input from other sources – other representations of the socio-cultural context.

It was argued in Chapter 6 that it is not inconsistent or contradictory to argue that the 'effects' of unconventional scripts may be more powerful than those of routine TV. Defying the everyday is in principle a much more noticeable activity than confirming it. If it is the case that TV influence is more detectable and more direct when going against the grain, the important question arises of whether the real culpability of the medium rests not so much on what it does, but in what it fails to do. And that is a judgement that I leave to the reader.

Conclusions

Attempting to demonstrate that television can be 'blamed' for causing 3, or 13, or 33 per cent of sex role stereotyping in developing children is a seductive but ultimately unproductive task. It is difficult to measure sex role beliefs and it is still more difficult to isolate the precise effects of any one environmental variable implicated in their development. I have argued in this book that measures of amount of viewing tell us very little about direct causal relationships, and it is conceivable that they may even lead us to overlook some effects which do occur. For example, I have speculated in this chapter that adolescence may be a period when individuals are likely to pay particular attention to television sex role information and in some cases try to relate it to their own lives; authoritative surveys (e.g. Comstock *et al.* 1978) show that during adolescence television viewing time *diminishes* relative to earlier periods. If my speculations about effects during this period are correct (and they are shared by other researchers into sex role development, e.g. Katz 1979), then clearly we need some more useful account of the relationship between viewer and medium than mere hours spent together.

In contrast to essentially unidirectional theories which assume that television *does something to* the viewer, I have argued that we need to develop theories which are both *social*, acknowledging that the viewer is located in an interpersonal and socio-cultural context within which he or she *does something with* televison, and *developmental*, acknowledging that the viewer's capacities to interpret and respond to television information will vary as a function of other attainments in the course of developing as a social-cognitive being. There are many gaps in such a framework but it promises a more fruitful approach to the study of children and television than theories which attribute causation uniquely to biology, environment, or individual reasoning.

Some of the problems discussed in this book may make it clear why the study of mass media effects is such a challenging and often frustratingly inconclusive area of social science research. Similarly, it will be transparent by now why the study of social development in childhood is one of the most demanding fields of psychology. Put these two together and we are confronted with very difficult issues to which we do not yet have all of the answers. It is not surprising that the answers do not promise to be as simple and as clear-cut as some early perspectives on television sex roles might lead us to expect, but we may at least be on the verge of asking better questions.

References

Abelson, R. P. (1976). Script processing in attitude formation and decision making. *In* Carroll, J. and Payne, J. W. (Eds), *Cognition and Social Behavior*. Hillsdale, New Jersey: Lawrence Erlbaum.

Anderson, D. R. and Levin, S. R. (1976). Young children's attention to 'Sesame Street'. *Child Development*, **47**, 806–811.

Anderson, D. R. and Lorch, E. P. (1983). Looking at television: action or reaction. *In* Bryant, J. and Anderson, D. R. (Eds), *Children's Understanding of Television. Research on Attention and Comprehension*. New York: Academic Press.

Anderson, D. R., Lorch, E. P., Field, D. E. and Sanders, J. (1981). The effects of TV program comprehensibility on preschool children's visual attention to television. *Child Development*, **52**, 151–157.

Archer, J. (1984). Gender roles as developmental pathways. *British Journal of Social Psychology*, **23**, 245–256.

Archer, J. and Lloyd, B. B. (1982). *Sex and Gender*. Harmondsworth: Penguin.

Aronoff, C. E. (1974). Sex roles and aging on TV. Summary in *Journal of Communication*, **2**, 127.

Ashmore, R. D. and Del Boca, F. K. (1979). Sex stereotypes and implicit personality theory: toward a cognitive-social psychological conceptualization. *Sex Roles*, **5**, 219–248.

Axelrad, D. M. (1976). Ring around collar-chain around her neck – proposal to monitor sex-role stereotyping in television advertising. *Hastings Law Journal*, **28**, 149–190.

Bandura, A. (1969). A social-learning theory of identificatory processes. *In* Goslin, D. A. (Ed.), *Handbook of Socialization Theory and Research*. Chicago: Rand McNally.

Bandura, A. (1977). *Social Learning Theory*. Englewood Cliffs, New Jersey: Prentice-Hall.

Bandura, A., Ross, D. and Ross, S. A. (1963). Imitation of film-mediated aggressive models. *Journal of Abnormal and Social Psychology*, **66**, 3–11.

Barcus, F. E. (1977). *Children's Television: An Analysis of Programming and Advertising*. New York: Praeger.

Barkley, R. A., Ullman, D. G., Otto, L. and Brecht, J. M. (1977). The effects of sex typing and sex appropriateness of modelled behavior on children's imitation. *Child Development*, **48**, 721–725.

BBC (1974). *Children as Viewers and Listeners. A Study by the BBC for its General Advisory Council*. London: British Broadcasting Council.

Bem, S. L. (1974). The measurement of psychological androgyny. *Journal of Consulting and Clinical Psychology*, **42**, 155–162.

Bem, S. L. (1983). Gender schema theory and its implications for child development: raising gender-aschematic children in a gender-schematic society. *Signs: Journal of Women in Culture and Society*, **8**, 598–616.

Berelson, B. (1952). *Content Analysis in Communication Research*. Glencoe, Illinois: Free Press.

Beuf, A. (1974). Doctor, lawyer, household drudge. *Journal of Communication*, **24**, 142–145.

Brooks-Gunn, J. and Matthews, W. S. (1979). *He & She. How Children Develop Their Sex-Role Identity*. Englewood Cliffs, New Jersey: Prentice-Hall.

Brown, D. G. (1956). Sex-role preference in young children. *Psychological Monographs*, **70**.

Busby, L. J. (1975). Sex-role research on the mass media. *Journal of Communication*, **25**, 107–131.

Butler, M. and Paisley, W. (1980). *Women and the Mass Media: Sourcebook for Research and Action*. New York: Human Sciences Press.

Chaffee, S. H. (1972). The interpersonal context of mass communication. *In* Kline, F. G. and Tichenor, P. J. (Eds) *Current Perspectives in Mass Communication Research*. Beverly Hills: Sage.

Chaffee, S. H. and Tims, A. R. (1976). Interpersonal factors in adolescent television use. *Journal of Social Issues*, **32**, 98–115.

Cheles-Miller, P. (1975). Reactions to marital roles in commercials. *Journal of Advertising Research*, **15**, 45–49.

Cobb, N. J., Stevens-Long, J. and Goldstein, S. (1982). The influence of televised models on toy preference in children. *Sex Roles*, **8**, 1075–1080.

Collins, W. A. (1983). Social antecedents, cognitive processing, and comprehension of social portrayals on television. *In* Higgins, E. T., Ruble, D. N. and Hartup, W. W. (Eds), *Social Cognition and Social Development: A Sociocultural Perspective*. Cambridge: Cambridge University Press.

Comstock, G., Chaffee, S., Katzman, N., McCombs, M. and Roberts, D. (1978). *Television and Human Behavior*. New York: Columbia University Press.

Constantinople, A. (1979). Sex-role acquisition: in search of the elephant. *Sex Roles*, **5**, 121–133.

Cordua, G. D., McGraw, K. O. and Drabman, R. S. (1979). Doctor or nurse: children's perception of sex-typed occupations. *Child Development*, **50**, 590–593.

Culley, J. A. and Bennett, R. (1976). Selling women, selling blacks. *Journal of Communication*, **26**, 160–178.

Davidson, E. S., Yasuna, M. and Tower, A. (1979). The effects of television cartoons on sex-role stereotyping in young girls. *Child Development*, **50**, 597–600.

Deaux, K. (1976). *The Behavior of Women and Men*. California: Wadsworth Publishing Company.

de Beauvoir, S. (1949). *The Second Sex*. London: New English Library. (*Trans.* H. M. Parshley; printed 1970).

De Fleur, M. (1964). Occupational roles as portrayed on television. *Public Opinion Quarterly*, **28**, 57–74.

Dohrmann, R. (1975). A gender profile of children's educational TV. *Journal of Communication*, **25**, 56–65.

Dominick, J. R. (1979). The portrayal of women in prime time, 1953–1977. *Sex Roles*, **5**, 405–411.

Dominick, J. R. and Rauch, G. (1972). The image of women in network TV commercials. *Journal of Broadcasting*, **16**, 259–265.

Dorr, A. (1980). When I was a child I thought as a child. In Withey, S. B. and Abeles, R. P. (Eds), *Television and Social Behavior: Beyond Violence and Children*. Hillsdale, New Jersey: Lawrence Erlbaum.

Dorr Leifer, A., Gordon, N. J. and Graves, S. B. (1974). Children's television: more than mere entertainment. *Harvard Educational Review*, **44**, 213–245.

Downing, M. (1974). Heroine of the daytime serial. *Journal of Communication*, **24**, 130–137.

Downs, A. C. (1981). Sex-role stereotyping on prime-time television. *Journal of Genetic Psychology*, **138**, 253–258.

Drabman, R. S., Robertson, S. J., Patterson, J. N., Jarvie, G. J., Hammer, D. and Cordua, G. (1981). Children's perception of media-portrayed sex roles. *Sex Roles*, **7**, 379–389.

Durkin, K. (1984). Children's accounts of sex-role stereotypes in television. *Communication Research*, **11**, 341–362.

Durkin, K. (1985a). Television and sex role acquisition 1: Content. *British Journal of Social Psychology*, 24, 101–113.

Durkin, K. (1985b). Television and sex role acquisition 2: Effects. *British Journal of Social Psychology*.

Durkin, K. (1985c). Television and sex role acquisition 3: Counterstereotyping. *British Journal of Social Psychology*.

Durkin, K. (in press). Sex roles and the mass media. In Hargreaves, D. J. and Colley, A. (Eds), *The Psychology of Sex Roles*. London: Harper & Row

Durkin, K. and Akhtar, P. (Forthcoming). Effects of a professionally produced counterstereotype programme on young school children's sex-role beliefs. Manuscript in preparation, Social Psychology Research Unit, University of Kent at Canterbury.

Durkin, K. and Hutchins, G. (1984). Challenging traditional sex-role stereotypes via careers education broadcasts: the reactions of young secondary school pupils. *Journal of Educational Television*, **10**, 25–33.

Eddings, B. M. (1980). Women in broadcasting (U.S.). *Women's Studies International Quarterly*, **3**, 1–13.

Eisenberg, N. (1983). Sex-typed toy choices: what do they signify. In Liss, M. B. (Ed.), *Social and Cognitive Skills. Sex Roles and Children's Play*. New York: Academic Press.

Eisenstock, B. (1984). Sex-role differences in children's identification with counterstereotypical televised portrayals. *Sex Roles*, **10**, 417–430.

Eiser, J. R. (1980). *Cognitive Social Psychology: A Guidebook to Theory and Research*. London: McGraw-Hill.

Emmerich, W., Goldman, K. S., Kirsh, B. and Sharabany, R. (1977). Evidence for a traditional phase in the development of gender constancy. *Child Development*, **48**, 930–936.

Fairweather, H. (1976). Sex differences in cognition. *Cognition*, **4**, 231–280.

Flerx, V. C., Fidler, D. S. and Rogers, R. W. (1976). Sex role stereotypes: Developmental aspects and early intervention. *Child Development*, **47**, 998–1007.

Frieze, I. H., Parsons, J. E., Johnson, P. B., Ruble, D. N. and Zellman, G. L. (1978). *Women and Sex Roles: A Social Psychological Perspective*. New York: Norton.

Frueh, T. and McGhee, P. E. (1975). Traditional sex role development and amount of time spent watching television. *Developmental Psychology*, **11**, 109.

Gable, J. (1984). Ageism: a new sales asset. *The Sunday Times*, 12 August, p. 35.

Gans, H. J. (1980). The audience for television – and in television research. In Withey, S. B. and Abeles, R. P. (Eds), *Television and Social Behavior: Beyond Violence and Children*. Hillsdale, New Jersey: Lawrence Erlbaum.

Geis, F. L., Brown, V., Jennings (Walstedt), J. and Porter, N. (1984). TV commercials as achievement scripts for women. *Sex Roles*, **10**, 513–525.

Gerbner, G., Gross, L., Morgan, M. and Signorielli, N. (1980). The 'mainstreaming' of America: Violence Profile No. 11. *Journal of Communication*, **30**, 10–29.

Gergen, K. J. and Gergen, M. M. (1981). *Social Psychology*. New York: Harcourt Brace Jovanovich.

Greenberg, B. S. (1982). Television and role socialization: an overview. *In* Pearl, D., Bouthilet, L. and Lazar, J. (Eds), *Television and Behavior: Ten Years of Scientific Progress and Implications for the Eighties*. Rockville, Maryland: NIMH.

Greenberg, B. S. and Reeves, B. (1976). Children and the perceived reality of television. *Journal of Social Issues*, **32**, 86–97.

Greenfield, P. M. (1984). *Mind and Media. The Effects of Television, Computers and Video Games*. London: Fontana.

Gross, L. and Jeffries-Fox, S. (1978). 'What do you want to be when you grow up, little girl?' *In* Tuchman, G., Daniels, A. and Benét, J. (Eds), *Hearth and Home: Images of Women in the Mass Media*. New York: Oxford University Press.

Gunter, B. and Wober, M. (1982). Television viewing and perceptions of women's roles on television and in real life. *Current Psychological Research*, **2**, 277–288.

Hamburg, D. A. and Lunde, D. T. (1966). Sex hormones in the development of sex differences in human behaviour. *In* Maccoby, E. E. (Ed.), *The Development of Sex Differences*. Stanford: Stanford University Press.

Harris, A. J. and Feinberg, J. F. (1977). Television and aging. Is what you see what you get? *The Gerontologist*, **17**, 464–468.

Hartley, R. E. (1959). Sex-role pressures and the socialization of the male child. *Psychological Reports*, **5**, 457–468.

Hennessee, J. and Nicholson, J. (1972). NOW says: TV commercials insult women. *New York Times Magazine*, May 28, pp. 13, 48–51.

Himmelweit, H. T., Oppenheim, A. N. and Vince, P. (1958). *Television and the Child: An Empirical Study of the Effect of Television on the Young*. Oxford: Oxford University Press.

Hobson, D. (1980). Housewives and the mass media. *In* Hall, S., Hobson, D., Lowe, A. and Willis, P. (Eds), *Culture, Media, Language*. London: Hutchinson.

Hoffman, L. W. (1977). Changes in family roles, socialization and sex differences. *American Psychologist*, **32**, 644–657.

Hoffman, M. L. (1983). Affective and cognitive processes in moral internalization. *In* Higgins, E. T., Ruble, D. N. and Hartup, W. W. (Eds), *Social Cognition and Social Development. A Sociocultural Perspective*. Cambridge: Cambridge University Press.

Hollenbeck, A. R. and Slaby, R. G. (1979). Infant visual and vocal responses to television. *Child Development*, **50**, 41–45.

Howitt, D. (1976). The effects of television on children. *In* Brown, R. (Ed.), *Children and Television*. London: Collier Macmillan.

Howitt, D. (1982). *Mass Media and Social Problems*. Oxford: Pergamon Press.

Howitt, D. and Cumberbatch, G. (1976). The parameters of attraction to mass media figures. *In* Brown, R. (Ed.), *Children and Television*. London: Collier Macmillan.

Huston, A. C., Greer, D., Wright, J. C., Welch, R. and Ross, R. (1984). Children's comprehension of televised formal features with masculine and feminine connotations. *Developmental Psychology*, **20**, 707–716.

Huston-Stein, A. and Friedrich, L. K. (1975). The effects of television content on young children. *In* Pick, A. D. (Ed.), *Minnesota Symposia on Child Psychology Vol. 9*. Minneapolis: University of Minnesota Press.

Huston-Stein, A. and Higgins-Trenk, A. (1977). The development of females: career and feminine role aspirations. *In* Baltes, P. B. (Ed.), *Life-Span Development and Behavior. Vol. I*. New York: Academic Press.

Hutt, C. (1972). *Males and Females*. Harmondsworth: Penguin.

Hutt, C. (1978). Sex-role differentiation in social development. *In* McGurk, H. (Ed.), *Issues in Childhood Social Development*. London: Methuen.

Janis, I. L. (1980). The influence of television on personal decision-making. *In* Withey, S. B. and Abeles, R. P. (Eds), *Television and Social Behavior: Beyond Violence and Children*. Hillsdale, New Jersey: Lawrence Erlbaum.

Johnston, J. and Ettema, J. S. (1982). *Positive Images: Breaking Stereotypes with Children's Television*. Beverly Hills and London: Sage.

Kalisch, B. J., Kalisch, P. A. and McHugh, M. (1981). Content analysis of film stereotypes of nurses. *International Journal of Women's Studies*, **3**, 515–530.

Kaniuga, N., Scott, T. and Gade, E. (1974). Working women portrayed on evening television programs. *Vocational Guidance Quarterly*, **23**, 134–137.

Katz, P. A. (1979). The development of female identity. *In* Kopp, C. B. (Ed.), *Becoming Female. Perspectives on Development*. New York: Plenum.

Kimball, M. M. (1977). Television and sex-role attitudes. Unpublished paper, cited in Morgan (1980).

Kington, M. (1983). *Moreover . . .* Harmondsworth: Penguin.

Knill, B. J., Pesch, M., Pursey, G., Gilpin, P. and Perloff, R. M. (1981). Still typecast after all these years? Sex role portrayals in television advertising. *International Journal of Women's Studies*, **4**, 497–506.

Kohlberg, L. (1966). A cognitive-developmental analysis of children's sex-role concepts and attitudes. *In* Maccoby, E. E. (Ed.), *The Development of Sex Differences*. Stanford: Stanford University Press.

Lemon, J. (1977). Women and blacks on prime-time television. *Journal of Communication*, **27**, 70–79.

Lemon, J. (1978). Dominant or dominated? Women on prime-time television. *In* Tuchman, G., Daniels, A. K. and Benét, J. (Eds), *Hearth and Home: Images of Women in the Mass Media*. New York: Oxford University Press.

Lepper, M. R. (1983). Social-control processes and the internalization of social values: an attributional perspective. *In* Higgins, E. T., Ruble, D. N. and Hartup, W. W. (Eds), *Social Cognition and Social Development. A Sociocultural Perspective*. Cambridge: Cambridge University Press.

Levinson, R. M. (1973). From Olive Oyl to Sweet Polly Purebread: Sex role stereotypes and televised cartoons. *Journal of Popular Culture*, **9**, 561–573.

List, J. A., Collins, W. A. and Westby, S. D. (1983). Comprehension and inferences from traditional and non-traditional sex-role portrayals on television. *Child Development*, **54**, 1579–1587.

Long, M. L. and Simon, R. J. (1974). The roles and statuses of women on children and family TV programs. *Journalism Quarterly*, **51**, 107–110.

Lyle, J. and Hoffman, H. R. (1976). Television viewing by pre-school-age children. *In* Brown, R. (Ed.), *Children and Television*. London: Collier Macmillan.

McArthur, L. Z. (1982). Judging a book by its cover: A cognitive analysis of the relationship between physical appearance and stereotyping. *In* Hastorf, A. H. and Isen, A. M. (Eds), *Cognitive Social Psychology*. Amsterdam: North Holland.

McArthur, L. Z. and Eisen, S. V. (1976). Television and sex-role stereotyping. *Journal of Applied Social Psychology*, **6**, 329–351.

McArthur, L. Z. and Resko, B. G. (1975). The portrayal of men and women in American television commercials. *Journal of Social Psychology*, **97**, 209–220.

McGhee, P. E. (1975). Television as a source of learning sex-role stereotypes. *In* Cohen, S. and Comiskey, T. J. (Eds), *Child Development. Contemporary Perspectives*. Illinois: Peacock Publishers.

McGhee, P. E. and Frueh, T. (1980). Television viewing and the learning of sex-role stereotypes. *Sex Roles*, **6**, 179–188.

McLeod, J. M. Fitzpatrick, M. A., Glynn, C. J. and Fallis, S. F. (1982). Television and social relations: Family influences and consequences for interpersonal behavior. *In* Pearl, D., Bouthilet, L. and Lazar, J. (Eds), *Television and Behavior: Ten Years of Scientific Progress and Implications for the Eighties. Volume 2: Technical Reviews*. Washington, D.C.: Government Printing Office.

McNeil, J. C. (1975). Feminism, femininity and the television series: A content analysis. *Journal of Broadcasting*, **3**, 259–271.

McQuail, D. (1976). Alternative models of television influence. *In* Brown, R. (Ed.), *Children and Television*. London: Collier Macmillan.

McQuail, D. (1983). *Mass Communication Theory: An Introduction*. London and Beverly Hills: Sage.

Maccoby, E. E. and Jacklin, C. N. (1974). *The Psychology of Sex Differences*. Stanford: Stanford University Press.

Manes, A. L. and Melnyk, P. (1974). Televised models of female achievement. *Journal of Applied Social Psychology*, **4**, 365–374.

Manstead, A. S. R. and McCulloch, C. (1981). Sex-role stereotyping in British television advertisements. *British Journal of Social Psychology*, **20**, 171–180.

Maracek, J., Piliavin, J., Fitzsimmons, E., Krogh, E., Leader, E. and Trudell, B. (1978). Women as TV experts: the voice of authority? *Journal of Communication*, **28**, 159–168.

Masters, J. C., Ford, M. E., Arend, R., Grotevant, H. D. and Clark, L. V. (1979). Modeling and labeling as integrated determinants of children's sex-typed imitative behavior. *Child Development*, **50**, 364–371.

Mayes, S. L. and Valentine, K. B. (1979). Sex role stereotyping in Saturday morning cartoon shows. *Journal of Broadcasting*, **23**, 41–50.

Messaris, P. and Sarett, C. (1981). On the consequences of television-related parent–child interaction. *Human Communication Research*, **7**, 226–244.

Meyer, B. (1980). The development of girls' sex-role attitudes. *Child Development*, **51**, 508–514.

Miller, M. M. and Reeves, B. (1976). Dramatic TV content and children's sex-role stereotypes. *Journal of Broadcasting*, **20**, 35–50.

Mischel, W. (1966). A social learning view of sex differences in behavior. *In* Maccoby, E. E. (Ed.), *The Development of Sex Differences*. Stanford: Stanford University Press.

Mischel, W. (1970). Sex-typing and socialization. *In* Mussen, P. H. (Ed.), *Carmichael's Manual of Child Psychology. Vol. 2*. New York: Wiley.

Mischel, W. (1976). *An Introduction to Personality. 2nd Edition*. New York: Holt, Rinehart & Winston.

Money, J. and Ehrhardt, A. A. (1972). *Man and Woman, Boy and Girl*. Baltimore: John Hopkins University Press.

Morgan, M. (1982). Television and adolescents' sex-role stereotypes: A longitudinal study. *Journal of Personality and Social Psychology*, **43**, 947–955.

Neisser, U. (1967). *Cognitive Psychology*. New York: Appleton-Century-Crofts.

Neisser, U. (1980). On social knowing. *Personality and Social Psychology Bulletin*, **6**, 601–605.

Nelson, K. (1981). Social cognition in a script framework. *In* Flavell, J. H. and Ross, L. (Eds), *Social Cognitive Development. Frontiers and Possible Futures*. Cambridge: Cambridge University Press.

Nelson, K. and Gruendel, J. (1981). Generalized event representations: basic building blocks of cognitive development. *In* Brown, A. and Lamb, M. (Eds), *Advances in Developmental Psychology. Vol. I*. Hillsdale; New Jersey: Lawrence Erlbaum.

Nicholson, J. (1984). *Men and Women: How Different Are They?* Oxford: Oxford University Press.

Nolan, J. D., Galst, J. P. and White, M. A. (1977). Sex bias on children's television programs. *Journal of Psychology*, **96**, 197–204.

O'Bryant, S. L. and Corder-Bolz, C. R. (1978). The effects of television on children's stereotyping of women's work roles. *Journal of Vocational Behavior*, **12**, 233–244.

O'Kelly, C. G. (1974). Sexism in children's television. *Journalism Quarterly*, **51**, 722–724.

Ounsted, C. and Taylor, D. C. (1972). The Y-chromosome message: a point of view. *In*

Ounsted, C. and Taylor, D. C. (Eds), *Gender Differences – Their Ontogeny and Significance*. London: Churchill.

Paludi, M. A. (1981). Sex-role discrimination among girls: Effect on IT Scale for Children scores. *Developmental Psychology*, **17**, 851–852.

Perloff, R. M. (1977). Some antecedents of children's sex-role stereotypes. *Psychological Reports*, **40**, 463–466.

Pingree, S. (1978). The effects of non-sexist television commercials and perceptions of reality on children's attitudes about women. *Psychology of Women Quarterly*, **2**, 262–277.

Pleck, J. H. (1976). The male sex role: definitions, problems, and sources of change. *Journal of Social Issues*, **32**, 155–164.

Poulos, R. W., Harvey, S. E. and Liebert, R. M. (1976). Saturday morning television: a profile of the 1974–75 children's season. *Psychological Reports*, **39**, 1047–1057.

Pyke, S. W. and Stewart, J. (1974). This column is about women: women and television. *Ontario Psychologist*, **6**, 66–69.

Reeves, B. and Miller, M. M. (1978). A multidimensional measure of children's identification with television characters. *Journal of Broadcasting*, **22**, 71–86.

Repetti, R. L. (1984). Determinants of children's sex-stereotyping: parental sex-role traits and television viewing. *Personality and Social Psychology Bulletin*, **10**, 457–468.

Roberts, E. J. (1982). Television and sexual learning in childhood. *In* Pearl, D., Bouthilet, L. and Lazar, J. (Eds), *Television and Behavior: Ten Years of Scientific Progress and Implications for the Eighties*. Rockville, Maryland: NIMH.

Roloff, M. E. (1981). Interpersonal and mass communication scripts. An interdisciplinary link. *In* Wilhoit, G. C. and de Bock, H. (Eds), *Mass Communication Review Yearbook 2*. Beverly Hills: Sage.

Rosenkrantz, P., Vogel, S., Bee, H., Broverman, I. and Broverman, D. M. (1968). Sex-role stereotypes and self-concepts in college students. *Journal of Consulting and Clinical Psychology*, **32**, 287–295.

Ross, L., Anderson, D. R. and Wisocki, P. A. (1982). Television viewing and adult sex-role attitudes. *Sex Roles*, **8**, 589–592.

Rubin, J. Z., Provenzano, F. J. and Luria, Z. (1974). The eye of the beholder: Parents' views on sex of newborns. *American Journal of Orthopsychiatry*, **44**, 512–519.

Ruble, D. N., Balaban, T. and Cooper, J. (1981). Gender constancy and the effects of sex-typed television toy commercials. *Child Development*, **52**, 667–673.

Salomon, G. (1979). *Interaction of Media, Cognition, and Learning*. San Francisco: Jossey-Bass.

Sayers, J. (1979). On the description of psychological sex differences. *In* Hartnett, O., Boden, G. and Fuller, M. (Eds), *Sex-Role Stereotyping*. London: Tavistock Publications Limited.

Sayers, J. (1982). *Biological Politics. Feminist and Anti-Feminist Perspectives*. London: Tavistock Publications.

Sayers, J. (in press). *Sexual Contradictions: Psychology, Psychoanalysis and Feminism*. London: Tavistock Publications.

Schank, R. and Abelson, R. (1977). *Scripts, Plans, Goals and Understanding. An Inquiry into Human Knowledge Structures*. Hillsdale, New Jersey: Lawrence Erlbaum.

Schramm, W., Lyle, J. and Parker, E. B. (1961). *Television in the Lives of our Children*. Stanford: Stanford University Press.

Seavey, C. A., Katz, P. A. and Zalk, S. R. (1975). Baby X: the effect of gender labels on adult responses to infants. *Sex Roles*, **1**, 103–109.

Seggar, J. F. and Wheeler, P. (1973). World of work on TV: ethnic and sex representation in TV drama. *Journal of Broadcasting*, **17**, 201–214.

Singer, J. L. and Singer, D. G. (1981). *Television, Imagination and Aggression: A Study of Preschoolers*. Hillsdale, New Jersey: Lawrence Erlbaum.

Slaby, R. G. and Frey, K. S. (1975). Development of gender constancy and selective attention to same-sex models. *Child Development*, **46**, 849–856.

Smith, C. and Lloyd, B. B. (1978). Maternal behavior and perceived sex of infant. *Child Development*, **49**, 1263–1265.

Spence, J. T. and Helmreich, R. L. (1978). *Masculinity and Femininity. Their Psychological Dimensions, Correlates, and Antecedents*. Austin: University of Texas Press.

Sprafkin, J. N. and Liebert, R. M. (1978). Sex-typing and children's television preferences. *In* Tuchman, G., Daniels, A. K. and Benét, J. (Eds), *Hearth and Home: Images of Women in the Mass Media*. New York: Oxford University Press.

Sternglanz, S. H. and Serbin, L. A. (1974). Sex role stereotyping in children's television programs. *Developmental Psychology*, **10**, 710–715.

Stone, V. (1972). Radio and television news directors and operations: An RTNDA survey. Research report presented at the International Conference of the Radio and Television News Directors Association, Nassau, Bahamas, 1972. Cited in Tan *et al.*, 1980.

Super, D. E. (1957). *The Psychology of Careers*. New York: Harper & Row.

Tajfel, H. (1981). *Human Groups and Social Categories*. Cambridge: Cambridge University Press.

Tan, A. S. (1979). TV beauty ads and role expectations of adolescent female viewers. *Journalism Quarterly*, **56**, 283–288.

Tan, A., Raudy, J., Huff, C. and Miles, J. (1980). Children's reactions to male and female newscasters' effectiveness and believability. *Quarterly Journal of Speech*, **66**, 201–205.

Tanner, J. M. (1972). Sequence, tempo, and individual variation in growth and development of boys and girls aged twelve to sixteen. *In* Kagan, J. and Coles, R. (Eds), *Twelve to Sixteen: Early Adolescence*. New York: Norton.

Tedesco, N. S. (1974). Patterns in prime time. *Journal of Communication*, **24** 119–124.

Thompson, S. K. (1975). Gender labels and early sex role development. *Child Development*, **46**, 339–347.

Tuchman, G. (1978). The symbolic annihilation of women by the mass media. *In* Tuchman, G., Daniels, A. and Benét, J. (Eds.), *Hearth and Home: Images of Women in the Mass Media*. New York: Oxford University Press.

Turiel, E. (1983). *The Development of Social Knowledge. Morality and Convention*. Cambridge: Cambridge University Press.

Turow, J. (1974). Advising and ordering: daytime, prime time. *Journal of Communication*, **24**, 138–141.

Ullian, D. Z. (1976). The development of conceptions of masculinity and femininity. *In* Lloyd, B. B. and Archer, J. (Eds), *Exploring Sex Differences*. London and New York: Academic Press.

Weigel, R. H. and Loomis, J. W. (1981). Televised models of female achievement revisited: Some progress, *Journal of Applied Social Psychology*, **11**, 58–63.

Welch, R. L., Huston-Stein, A., Wright, J. C. and Plehal, R. (1979). Subtle sex-role cues in children's commercials. *Journal of Communication*, **29**, 202–209.

Whipple, T. W. and Courtney, A. E. (1980). How to portray women in TV commercials. *Journal of Advertising Research*, **20**, 53–59.

Williams, F., LaRose, R. and Frost, F. (1981). *Children, Television and Sex-Role Stereotyping*. New York: Praeger.

Williams, J. E. and Best, D. L. (1982). *Measuring Sex Stereotypes*. Beverly Hills: Sage.

Williams, J. E., Bennett, S. M. and Best, D. L. (1975). Awareness and expression of sex stereotypes in young children. *Developmental Psychology*, **11**, 635–642.

Williams, T. M. (1981). How and what do children learn from television? *Human Communication Research*, **7**, 180–192.

Wilson, E. O. (1975). *Sociobiology: The New Synthesis*. Cambridge, Massachusetts: Harvard University Press.

Wilson, E. O. (1978). *On Human Nature*. Cambridge, Massachusetts: Harvard University Press.

Winick, M. P. and Winick, C. (1979). *The Television Experience: What Children See.* Beverly Hills: Sage Publications.

Withey, S. B. (1980). An ecological, cultural, and scripting view of television and social behavior. *In* Withey, S. B. and Abeles, R. P. (Eds), *Television and Social Behavior: Beyond Violence and Children.* Hillsdale, New Jersey: Lawrence Erlbaum.

Withey, S. B. and Abeles, R. P. (1980) (Eds). *Television and Social Behavior: Beyond Violence and Children.* Hillsdale, New Jersey: Lawrence Erlbaum.

Zuckerman, D. M., Singer, D. G. and Singer, J. L. (1980). Children's television viewing, racial and sex-role attitudes. *Journal of Applied Social Psychology,* **10**, 281–294.

Author Index

Subject Index